The
Official American Youth Soccer Organization Handbook

**Rules, Regulations, Skills, and
Everything Else Kids, Parents,
and Coaches Need to
Participate in Youth Soccer**

Vincent Fortanasce,
Lawrence Robinson, and
John Ouellette,
National Coach/Technical Director

Illustrations by Risé Reading

FIRESIDE
Published by Simon & Schuster
New York London Toronto Sydney Singapore

FIRESIDE
Rockefeller Center
1230 Avenue of the Americas
New York, NY 10020

Copyright © 2001 by The American Youth Soccer Organization
Illustrations copyright © 2001 by Risé Reading

FIRESIDE and colophon are registered trademarks
of Simon & Schuster, Inc.

The American Youth Soccer Organization's name,
mark, and all associated trademarks and logotypes
are owned by AYSO.

For information regarding special discounts for bulk purchases,
please contact Simon & Schuster Special Sales at 1-800-456-6798
or business@simonandschuster.com

Designed by Christine Weathersbee

Manufactured in the United States of America

1   3   5   7   9   10   8   6   4   2

Library of Congress Cataloging-in-Publication Data

American Youth Soccer Organization.
The official American Youth Soccer Organization handbook :
rules, regulations, skills, and everything else kids, parents,
and coaches need to participate in youth soccer /
Vincent Fortanasce, Lawrence Robinson, and John Ouellette;
illustrations by Risé Reading.
p.   cm.
Includes index.
1. Soccer for children—United States—Handbooks, manuals, etc.
2. Soccer for children—Coaching—United States—Handbooks,
manuals, etc.   I. Fortanasce, Vincent.   II. Robinson, Lawrence
(Lawrence John).   III. Ouellette, John.   IV. Title.
GV944.2 A52 2001
796.334'083—dc21   2001040119
ISBN 0-7432-1384-X

ACKNOWLEDGMENTS

Thanks to everyone at the American Youth Soccer Organization, especially Cathy Ferguson, Mark Valdez, Kim Lewis, Eric Veach, and Mark Alch for their invaluable help in writing this book, and Doris Cooper at Simon & Schuster for such a great editing job.

*For soccer players everywhere and
those who love to watch them*

CONTENTS

FOREWORD

As with great soccer, this book was a team effort. There are three authors listed on the cover, but we elected to pool our knowledge and experiences of youth soccer. Each incident recounted in the book actually happened, to at least one of us, more often than not to all three of us: Lawrence as a player, Vince as a parent and coach, and me as, well, as just about everything—from player, parent, coach, and referee, to distributor of oranges at halftime, to national coach of the most respected youth soccer organization in the United States.

Working as a team is as crucial off the soccer field as it is on. Little can be achieved in soccer or in life without the co-operation, hard work, and loyalty of others. So I would like to thank all my teammates at AYSO for their continued support of all our youth soccer programs and for their contribution to this project in particular. Our goal was to create a document that would not only detail the rules and regulations of soccer but also provide an understanding of the subtleties and nuances of the world's game and maybe help a few baffled parents understand their child's passion for what is still an unfamiliar sport to many.

Enjoy the read and enjoy the experience of youth soccer.

—*John Ouellette*
AYSO National Coach/Technical Director

INTRODUCTION:

The Beautiful Game

That beautiful game I love so well,
the game I live to play . . .

—Pelé

We are obsessed. And we have been since the first time we kicked a leather ball. By the time Lawrence was 5, for example, he was playing every evening after school with the neighborhood kids on a thin strip of grass that fell away in an alarmingly steep slope beyond his backyard fence. "We threw coats or sweaters down as goalposts," he remembers, "and played until dusk, when my mother's calls became too loud and insistent to ignore."

John's parents proudly remember how conscientious he was as a youngster, always arriving at elementary school early. "I never told them that all the kids met up every morning to play soccer." The game, consisting of a swarm of kids chasing a ratty tennis ball around the school playground, started before their first class, resumed at recess, and concluded during lunch. "It seemed that there was always a soccer game to be played."

Vince played for the elementary school team, the Cub Scout team, and a Saturday morning team whose name he can't quite remember. Then there was high school. Because of the size and reputation of the school, making the junior varsity team at the age of 14 held all the prestige of playing for one's country. "When I pulled that crisp polyester over my head for the first time," he says, "I felt like Pelé preparing to play for Brazil or Cruyff for Holland."

Lawrence recently met up with two of his closest friends in Los Angeles, and as they so often do, they reminisced about their years playing for the Danbury Boys Under-10s (U-10) through Under-16s (U-16). Richard ("Babs") is now a farmer. Back then he was the team's striker (primary goal scorer), a player best described simply as "an enigma" in front of goal. Dave, on the other hand, was a more consistent performer, usually beside Lawrence in defense, who went on to become a successful broker on Wall Street.

They all remember those Sunday afternoons with nothing but warmth—which means that youth soccer played the role it was meant to in their lives. They don't have mantlepieces littered with trophies or careers as professional players to look back on. They don't even have memories of winning many games. But what they do have are bonds of friendship that were formed on the soccer field and that have remained unbroken by time or geography. The best we can wish for any child playing youth soccer today is that in 25 years he or she will be able to say the same about their childhood teammates.

Groups of men and women, boys and girls, kicking a leather ball around a rectangular patch of land may seem like a silly pursuit to some. But the game of soccer has a way of generating such emotional intensity in those it touches that each game becomes a brief reflection of the muddled blend of drama, competitiveness, joy, and tragedy that saturate that other silly pursuit: the game of life.

Soccer, football, *futbol, futebol, calcio, fussball, fußbal, voetbol*—call it what you will, no other sport has the rich history or heritage to match "the beautiful game." No other sport breeds the passion, the insanity, the ecstasy, or the despair. Forget the hooligan reputation of a minority of soccer supporters—that's a social problem that has nothing to do with sport; ignore the allegations that it's a game for wimpy, bespectacled geeks—most soccer players, men and women, are supremely fit athletes; and dismiss the notion that the game is un-American—it's certainly no less American than golf.

Soccer is a wonderful pastime, an unstructured, flowing game that at its best blurs the line between sport and art. There's an intrinsic balletic quality to a sweeping passing move that carries the ball from one end of the field to the other and climaxes in a perfectly executed volley or a crisp diving header on goal. No, the scoring in soccer isn't as high as in other American sports, but that's part of the appeal. The scarcity value increases the importance of every goal, every missed shot, every fingertip save. The fact that goals are rarer and harder-earned than runs in baseball or points in basketball adds to the excitement and anticipation every time the ball is played in close to goal.

So, it's no wonder that today, more kids in America play soccer than any other youth sport. The Soccer Industry Council of America estimates that more than 26 million children under the age of 18 will play soccer at least once in 2001. More than 4 million kids are registered to play with

American youth soccer organizations, half a million more than with Little League, and that number is increasing at an annual rate of 8 to 10 percent. The sport is no longer reserved for first- and second-generation Americans, the sons of immigrants clinging to a tradition from their homeland. It's a game for everyone, a philosophy that the American Youth Soccer Organization, or AYSO, has taken to heart. Boys and girls are not registered on their merits as soccer players, but rather according to their interest and commitment.

"Enthusiasm," said the great Pelé, "is everything." To that end, the objectives of AYSO are to enthusiastically teach, promote, and cultivate youth soccer in the United States and to develop American youngsters in both body and character. Winning always comes second to enjoyment. With the beautiful game, everyone plays and everyone has fun.

Whether you're already a devoted soccer aficionado or, like more than 70 percent of AYSO's parents and volunteers, you've had little or no previous contact with the sport, this book is for you. It's an ideal reference to the game of soccer, its rules and the philosophies and regulations of the American Youth Soccer Organization. We hope it will also stand as a testament to a group of kids half a lifetime ago who learned the most valuable lesson that youth soccer has to teach: The results soon fade from memory, but the fun and the friendships can last forever.

Chapter 1

A Soccer Philosophy: Welcome to AYSO

Through soccer, kids are able to gain
self-confidence, develop a healthy attitude
toward competition, create long-lasting
friendships, and improve their physical health.

—Dan Calichman,
soccer pro and AYSO spokesperson

The year 1964 was memorable for many reasons. Lyndon Johnson was reelected president in a landslide victory; the U.S. military launched attacks on North Vietnam; race riots erupted in Harlem and other neighborhoods across the country; the Olympic Games were held in Tokyo; Cassius Clay defeated Sonny Liston to become World Heavyweight Champion; UCLA won its first national title in college basketball; and in the World Series, St. Louis beat the New York Yankees, 4–3. Meanwhile, in a small residential garage in the quiet Los Angeles suburb of Torrance, a group of soccer parents, frustrated at the lack of youth soccer teams available for their kids, assembled a roster of 125 players and formed a nonprofit organization they christened the American Youth Soccer Organization, or AYSO. The founders spent long hours huddled in the tiny garage determining a set of five philosophies that would guide their organization and protect the well-being of all the participants. These were the following:

1. Everyone Plays.
2. Balanced Teams.
3. Open Registration.
4. Positive Coaching.
5. Good Sportsmanship.

In the ensuing years, U.S. presidents came and went, peace descended over Vietnam, Cassius Clay became Muhammed Ali and retired, and the idea of St. Louis beating the Yankees in the World Series became almost unthinkable. Amidst it all, AYSO has evolved into a vibrant national organization with more than 630,000 players and 250,000 volunteers, and unprecedented influence over the development of youth soccer in the United States. And while AYSO's founders quickly outgrew the suburban garage in Torrance, the five philosophies determined in 1964 endured and now seem timeless.

The Philosophies

AYSO programs are open to all children from the ages of 4 years 6 months to U-19 players who love to play soccer. The organization offers training programs for players, coaches, referees, and volunteers designed to promote a fun-packed, family environment based on AYSO's five philosophies.

Everyone Plays

The goal of AYSO is for kids to play soccer, so each child who registers, regardless of ability, is guaranteed to play at least half of every game. In AYSO *everyone plays* because children learn skills, teamwork, and sportsmanship, and develop confidence and self-esteem by playing, not by being spectators.

In our day, the coach recruited and selected players, which was fine only if you had an experienced coach and a winning team. The Danbury Boys' Coach Gravett was certainly well-meaning. He gave up every Wednesday evening for training and every Sunday afternoon for the games. It saddens Lawrence now to remember how unappreciative he and his teammates were of the time and effort this man put into the team. But the truth was, for all his good intentions, the coach was bordering on the clueless when it came to coaching and organizing a soccer team.

Inevitably, the results gradually deteriorated throughout his first season, as did the enthusiasm of many of the players. By his second season in charge, they were struggling to field 11 players every week and rarely had enough kids turn up to provide us with the luxury of substitutes. Consequently, the policy "Everyone plays" was embraced by Coach Gravett and the Danbury Boys with all the necessity of a lifesaver for drowning man. But that is the key to why Lawrence and his friends enjoyed their time at Danbury Boys so much. Regardless of their abilities, they always got to play.

The AYSO founders knew how crucial the philosophy

"Everyone Plays" was to the acceptance of the organization. Kids flock to play soccer because it's fun to play. "Soccer involves movement, athleticism," notes John. "Players can't learn these skills sitting on the bench watching. Soccer can only be learned by *doing*." Games should be seen as an extension of practice sessions—further opportunities for the players to learn. Everyone has more fun when everyone plays.

Balanced Teams

Since games are more fun when the teams are of equal ability, every AYSO region sets up teams as evenly balanced as possible. Team balancing dates back to AYSO's first season, when the 50 or so players who showed up on registration day were simply distributed randomly. After a few friendly scrimmages, adjustments were made to assure the teams were comparable in talent.

"Balanced Teams" means competitive, interesting games for all who play and watch.

Winning 3–2 leaves youngsters with a greater sense of achievement than winning 7–0, for example. The more effort victory takes, the greater the sense of accomplishment. It's certainly better for the losing players to be defeated by only a narrow margin. With Danbury Boys, we were on the wrong end of 3–2 and 7–0 score games many times. No matter how much we loved playing the game, how much fun we had just being on the field, when people asked the score, it wasn't too painful to say, "We lost 3–2. We were unlucky." The same story never quite rang true when we had lost 7–0 or 8–0.

When teams are leading or trailing by so many goals, the effort and determination of players on both teams starts to wane. Players on the losing team know that with 10 minutes left they're never going to be able to score 7 goals to tie the game, so often they give up trying. Similarly, players on the winning team know that the game is already won, so there's no incentive for them to exert themselves any further and they coast through the remaining minutes. However, if the game is tied at 2–2, for example, or close at 3–2 with 10 minutes left, there's still everything to play for and every player has to maintain 100 percent effort. At the final whistle, win or lose, every player can take satisfaction in having played his or her heart out for the whole game.

Open Registration

AYSO has sign-ups, not tryouts, and does not restrict membership on the basis of talent, race, religion, gender, financial status, or any type of belief or attitude. Every child may register to play. Unlike Little League, kids can sign up with their parents in any community they choose, not only the one they live in.

In the early years, open registration had one very questionable provision: AYSO was open only to boys. But that inequity ended in 1971, when the girls program was started. With the initiation of the VIP (Very Important Player) program for kids with special needs and the Team-Up program for the economically disadvantaged, today the open registration policy is truly open to all.

Open registration complements the "Everyone Plays" philosophy. Regardless of sex, race, financial status, physical or mental abilities, every child has a place to play soccer.

Positive Coaching

AYSO promotes coaching through encouragement rather than criticism. Positive coaching is the glue that holds AYSO philosophies together and creates an atmosphere both in games and in practices where children feel comfortable taking risks and trying new skills and techniques without an overriding fear of failure. "Mistakes happen as part of the learning process," says Vince. "If children are to develop as players and people, they must be assured that they will not be snapped at for every mistake."

Coach Webber once told John's parents that if he kept working hard, he had a shot at making it as a professional player. John doubts if the coach really meant what he said, but it made his parents proud and gave him a welcome boost of confidence.

Coach Gravett walked over to Lawrence after he had just dribbled the ball through the opposition midfield and scored with a scorching 30-yard drive. He was more concerned that he had left his position in the center of defense. "Very good," he mumbled. "But don't do that again."

At the end of the U-12 season, even though John's team hadn't won anything, Coach Webber presented all the players with an engraved plaque and thanked them for their effort and hard work. It remains the only soccer trophy John has ever won.

After Babs struggled to score goals for several matches, Coach Gravett asked Lawrence to partner with Babs in attack. It was the first time Lawrence had played in that position, and he managed to score 4 goals even though they ultimately lost 6–4. "You'll have to go back in defense next week," Coach Gravett said to Lawrence after the game. "You can't score as many goals as you can stop."

It shouldn't come as a surprise to anyone that Coach Webber achieved more success with his players. Positive coaching means instructing without condemning; praising the individual but correcting the group; displaying good sportsmanship; and, in general, setting a good example for the players.

Good Sportsmanship

AYSO has active programs aimed at creating good sports on the field, on the sidelines, and far away from any playing ground.

The U.S. National Women's Team at the 2000 Olympic Games in Sydney, Australia, demonstrated the most vivid portrayal of good sportsmanship I can recall in recent times. The women of Team USA had already established themselves as great champions and gracious victors of the 1999 Women's World Cup, but in Sydney they tasted defeat after a stirring final against Norway. After the game, the U.S. players all turned and cheered the Norwegian team. It was a class act.

During the medal ceremony, Mia Hamm encouraged her teammates to be as proud of their accomplishments in winning silver as they were of winning gold four years earlier. "Heads up," she urged them.

When the final whistle blows, you no longer have any control over the result. All the missed chances, the silly mistakes, the decisions that went against you count for nothing. All you can control is the way you react. That's the attitude Team USA adopted at the Olympics.

Good sportsmanship is always more important than winning.

Chapter 2

The Team

Part of the beauty of soccer is its simplicity. All you need is a field, a ball, two teams, and a referee. The field is a little larger than the size of a football field, smaller for younger players, and the game is played in two halves, although AYSO mandates quarter breaks within each half to allow for player substitutions under the "Everyone Plays" philosophy.

A full-sided team has a maximum of 11 players on the field at any one time, although games can be played with as few as 3 on each team, which allows players more touches on the ball and enables them to learn ball control, passing, and shooting skills quickly.

Being a good teammate is [trying] to sprint down a ball that everyone thinks is going out of bounds. But you go after it anyway and you get it. Maybe you don't make a great cross with it to win the game, but you pushed yourself beyond what you thought you could.

—Mia Hamm

Being a team player is important, not only in soccer but in life. The ability to build relationships with others through cooperation, respect, and unselfish behavior is as valuable in the boardroom, on the factory floor, and at home as it is on the soccer field. Nothing in life is as important or rewarding as the forming of human relationships.

On the soccer field, kids soon learn the value of cooperation and teamwork. There's no one player, no matter how good she is, who can win a soccer game single-handedly. It takes every player on the team playing with commitment and enthusiasm for a team to be successful.

One Danbury Boys U-16 game has stayed in Lawrence's mind as vividly as any other. Eight or nine of the team had grown up together, playing together every season from the U-10 level. This particular game was an away game against the top-of-the-league team on a miserable, rainy Sunday afternoon. The usual reliable group of 9 players turned up, but the rest of the team clearly decided their time was better spent indoors, not out in the winter downpour. Rather than forfeiting the game because they couldn't field a starting 11, the 9 of them decided to play and give it their best shot.

They packed the defense with the hope of keeping the score down and maybe catching the opposing team on the break for a goal or two. But it was not to be. Their opponents were too good, and the game turned into a rout. Dave even suffered the embarrassment of scoring an own goal when he deflected a shot past his own goalkeeper and into the net. "I helped him up from the muddy goal mouth and told him we were already losing by so many that I didn't think they needed our help in scoring any more," remembers Lawrence. "He laughed and we walked back to the center circle to take yet another kickoff."

"I can't remember for certain the final score—something like 9 or 10–0—but what I do remember are the words of the referee after the game. As we trudged off the field, he called us over and said that in all his years as a youth soccer referee he had never seen a team play with such a great attitude. We never stopped smiling, and we never stopped trying, even though we had no chance of winning. When Dave scored that humiliating own goal, the rest of the team didn't criticize him for making a mistake. They just picked the ball out of the net and kept on playing.

"The referee shook each of our hands and told us we were a credit to both Coach Gravett and to the league. I forget the names of the players who didn't show up that afternoon, but I can name every one of those who did," Lawrence recalls. Twenty years later that same team spirit remains. "Some of those players remain my closest friends, and even though we live thousands of miles apart, dotted around the globe, we speak every few weeks and see each other as often as possible. Whatever mishaps have befallen each of us in the intervening years, we have always been able to rely on each other. We're as much a team now as we were then." And, as ever in life, it hasn't always been a winning team. But you learn more about a teammate who commiserates with you after you put the ball in your own net than one who only congratulates you for scoring at the right end.

Teamwork

When your child decides to join a team, it means he has committed herself to being part of a group, a group that is aiming to achieve the same goals. Not everyone can be the captain, the star player, or the leading scorer. But each member of the team has an important contribution to make. The star striker can only score if her teammates play the ball into the right place at the right time. No striker scores goals without help from her teammates.

As a coach, Vince never allowed his players to criticize each other. "There's no place on a soccer team for either a player who is jealous of a more talented teammate or one who becomes angry at a teammate who makes too many mistakes," he says. When a very talented player on the opposing team kept dribbling the ball through Vince's team's defense, rather than criticize the defender charged with marking (guarding) her, Vince encouraged all his defenders to back each other up every time this opposing player started to dribble toward one of them. Similarly, if the player received the ball in midfield, it was up to Vince's midfield players to stop her before she got as far as the defense. In other words, he made defending against that player a team responsibility. That way, if the player kept scoring goals, it was the team's fault, not an individual's. Likewise, if the player was prevented from scoring, it became the team's achievement rather than an individual's.

The defender who regularly wanders out of position leaving his or her goalkeeper exposed or the petulant, ill-disciplined midfielder who keeps getting sent off in games, leaving the team to finish the game a player short, are playing for themselves, not the team. The talented player who hogs the ball instead of passing to his teammates usually succeeds only in making his teammates angry and frustrated.

The skillful but greedy striker, for example, is almost a cliché in soccer. We've all seen them. To say that the Danbury Boys striker Babs fit this mold may be a little unfair—

we don't believe anyone would ever have described him as skillful. He was certainly a greedy player, though. Babs always took the shot whenever he was close to the goal, even when a teammate was in a better position to score if only he had passed the ball.

The defenders' frustration at Babs for being greedy and missing easy chances was matched only by his frustration at their awful defending. But that's the crux of teamwork. Neither kids nor pros can play every position at once. They have to rely on their teammates to do their jobs. And of course, they're going to make mistakes, just as every player does at all levels. As Sir Alex Ferguson, the famed manager of the English team Manchester United, once said, "Trust begins with understanding the other players' roles within the team. That lays the foundations for respecting each other and developing camaraderie."

Players can either get angry and annoyed with a teammate when he or she makes mistakes, which will only make the offending player feel even worse, or they can smile, pat their teammate on the back, and get on with the game.

Coaches and parents must remember:

1. Ridiculing or making fun of a teammate who makes a mistake only damages a team. Players who score an own goal or miss an easy chance or give away possession that leads to the opposition scoring know they've made a mistake and don't need their teammates rubbing it in. This will only erode their self-confidence and increase the likelihood they'll make other mistakes as the game progresses.

2. Every player is an equal partner in the team and so should put in equal effort and share equally in the team's success or failure. Whatever a child's posi-

tion on the team, she shares the blame if the team is thrashed by ten goals and, likewise, shares the credit for winning the championship. Every player is in it together, win, lose, or draw.

Coaches lead the way by demonstrating through example. Praise the individual, criticize the group.

What Makes a Team Player?

The best player is always a team player. These are some attributes of team players:

1. He is always willing to use individual skills when he needs to but also quick to put his talents at the disposal of other players on his team.
2. She works hard for the team, even when the game isn't going so well, doing things like turning a bad pass from a teammate into a good one.
3. Working hard for the team also means doing things away from the ball, like running into space to make it easier for a teammate to find him with a pass or dragging his marker (guard) away from the ball to create space for a teammate to run into.
4. She encourages teammates and acknowledges every player's role within the team, which helps develop a teammate's self-confidence, boosts her performance, and in turn benefits the team.

Great teams are not necessarily the ones packed with the best players. In fact, one of the great things about soccer is that those who play better as a team often beat the teams with the best players. Great teamwork in soccer can often triumph over individual skill.

Developing Teamwork

Developing teamwork doesn't happen with a single practice session or a single game but rather evolves throughout a season. Coaches need to:

1. Make every player on the team feel that he is making a meaningful contribution to the team. Praise defenders as much and as often as forwards. Praise good tackles, passes, or interceptions as much as goals.
2. Encourage players to congratulate each other for a good pass or a well-timed tackle and have them continually talking to each other, calling for the ball, warning each other of opposition players approaching, congratulating each other's efforts, and commiserating with each other about mistakes. Silence is for the classroom, not the soccer field.
3. Discourage anger, jealousy, or the tendency for skillful players to make fun of their less talented teammates. Set a ground rule that no player on your team is allowed to criticize another and regularly remind your players of that.
4. Mix up the starting players, try not to end the game with the same players who started it.

Win or lose, Vince always bought his team ice cream after a game. "It gives the players a chance to unwind together before they go their separate ways after a game." If, during the season, the players started to lose their enthusiasm for the training sessions, he would cancel practice and take the players to a skateboard park or to see a Major League Soccer game or to play tennis. This broke the monotony and helped the girls get to know each other away from soccer.

Lawrence remembers Coach Gravett trying something similar to instill team unity and spirit in his squad of players. And it ultimately proved successful. One evening the players arrived at the clubhouse to discover that Coach Gravett had elected to cancel training and replace it with a hastily arranged team building session that took the curious form of a "surprise" disco. A net full of semi-inflated balloons hung from the clubhouse ceiling and a couple of colored lights flashed intermittently to the tinny sounds of classic show tunes. Studio 54 it wasn't.

As ever with Coach Gravett, though, it was a well-meant gesture. Unfortunately, the concept of a surprise disco is inherently flawed. Other than Coach Gravett's 11-year-old niece, who served us bowls of chips and cups of flat soda, there were no girls there. And, for adolescents weaned on the music of The Clash, David Bowie, and Depeche Mode, a static-filled version of "Surrey with the Fringe on Top" didn't exactly have us bopping around the dance floor. Instead, the evening deteriorated into a dozen or so 15-year-old boys huddling in one corner of a creaking, wooden shed, trying to shield themselves against a bitter draft.

Coach Gravett wandered behind us, inexplicably wearing a pair of bright red soccer boots that he had carefully filed the molded studs off. He was the quintessential embarrassing parent, swaying out of time to the music with exaggerated enthusiasm, urging us to "get on down" or "feel the groove" or some other such expression that he thought would help him identify with his young charges.

Maybe it was the shared experience of surviving such adverse conditions, or perhaps cunning reverse psychology on the part of Coach Gravett, but as we left the clubhouse that night, there was a distinct change in the atmosphere between the players. We had bonded and were closer than ever.

Here are other activities AYSO coaches do to develop team spirit and camaraderie:

1. One coach remembers his players even when it's not soccer season, by sending them all Christmas or holiday cards.
2. Another coach has her team perform charitable work one day every season. It focuses the players on a common goal (helping the less fortunate) away from any kind of competitive environment.
3. Another coach makes a name tag for each player at the start of the season with the team logo inscribed on it.

It's not just coaches who can help to instill teamwork. Parents can nurture camaraderie and team play by remembering the following:

1. Encourage your child to thank his teammates if he scores a goal. Remind him, if he walks off the field at the end of the game bragging about a goal that he made, that he was able to score that goal only thanks to the work of his teammates. Suggest he go over and thank them for setting it up for him.

2. Urge your child to show compassion for a player who makes a mistake. After a game, if one player has made a mistake and is obviously feeling bad about it, ask your child how she would feel if she had made the mistake. Remind her to go over and offer her sympathy and to tell the player that no one feels angry or upset with her.

3. Emphasize to your child that all positions on the team are important. If your kid is the star of team, remind him that he can't win games on his own, that he needs every one of his teammates to be successful. If your child is less talented than the rest of the team, build his confidence by pointing out all the positive things he achieved during the game. Make your child feel good about himself whether he is the star striker or the reserve goalkeeper.

4. Help your child appreciate the roles of the other players on the team. Remind her that forwards can't score goals without midfielders setting up the chances and that scoring goals won't win games unless the defenders and goalkeeper manage to prevent the opposition from scoring.

Commitment

Commitment, discipline, and accountability also play a vital role in building teamwork. As much as John loved soccer and being part of a team, there was the occasional Sunday when he just didn't feel like playing or a Wednesday when he didn't want to train. "Maybe I was a little under the weather or had a lot of homework. Whatever the reason, my parents always insisted that I had made a commitment to the team and now had to honor that commitment, whether I felt like it or not."

The worst thing parents can do is to indulge and encourage such apathy. John never once regretted his parents forcing him to turn up for a game. But he knows for sure he would have regretted it if they hadn't. That sense of commitment has stayed with him into adulthood. "If I say I'll do something, I'll do it, and if I ever want to change my mind or get the urge to wangle my way out of a commitment, I always picture my mother's scornful expression and hear her saying, 'You've made a commitment. Friends don't let friends down.' "

Parents should discourage their child from quitting a team unless the child has good reason. If a child genuinely doesn't like soccer and wants to quit, make sure he or she replaces it with another physical activity. Perseverance and overcoming obstacles are important lessons a child can learn from participating in youth soccer. Teammates need to be able to rely on each other—confident that they'll come to practice as well as compete in games, and that they'll all give 100 percent effort all the time. If a child still insists on quitting the team, have the child explain the reason to the coach himself in order to teach him accountability.

Not everyone can be a great player, and not everyone can play in a successful team. But everyone can play a meaningful role in a team and reap the benefits of companionship and mutual esteem.

Positions on the Team

Soccer is one of the few sports where physical size isn't important—unlike in football or basketball, small players can often get the better of taller, stronger players. Maradona, for example, was only 5 foot 6 inches, but he dribbled the ball past no end of hulking, 6-foot-plus defenders.

There are no specific physical requirements for any particular position on the soccer field. It helps to be tall if you're a goalkeeper (taller players have more reach when diving to save shots or jumping up to grab high balls), but positional awareness and agility are worth more than a few extra inches. It helps to be fast if you're a winger, but an ability to make accurate, in-swinging crosses negates the need to run past opposing fullbacks. For every tall, strong striker that's a force in the air, there's a better one who is half the size but has a great spring in his step. For every stocky, well-balanced midfielder, there's a better one who is thin and gangly. For every lightning-quick defender, there's a superior one with half the pace but a better understanding of the game.

Kids discover their best position by trying them all out. Never listen to people who say that you're too small, too heavy, or too slow for a certain position. There's always an example that will prove them wrong.

Tall, short, fast, or slow, soccer teams normally consist of players in four primary positions.

The Goalkeeper

Also known as the "keeper," the goalkeeper is responsible for guarding the team's goal, blocking and saving shots to prevent the opposing team from scoring. The goalkeeper is the only player on the team allowed to use his hands and arms, although only within the designated penalty area. If he ventures beyond the penalty area, he can, like the rest of the outfield players, only use his legs, head, and torso to control or pass the ball.

A goalkeeper's allies are:

1. Agility
2. Mental toughness
3. Decisiveness
4. Lightning-quick reactions

The idea that it's just the fat kids or the nerdy introverts who play goalie in youth soccer is ludicrous. Goalkeeping is tough. It takes a special character to play in goal. There's nowhere for a keeper to hide—he's the last line of defense. Make a mistake as an outfield player, and there's a good chance one of your teammates can cover for you. Make a mistake as a keeper and the whole team pays. So a goalkeeper needs to have a thick skin and not be frightened of making a mistake.

A goalkeeper needs to have all the skills of an outfield player as well as those unique to his position. Coaches at youth level should encourage every outfield player to play keeper some time—if only so the whole team appreciates the special pressures that accompany the position. Any player that decides to play goalkeeper regularly also needs to develop his footwork, ball control, and passing skills as well, since keepers are sometimes caught outside the penalty area where they're unable to use their hands.

Lawrence played in goal for Danbury Boys on one occasion when Phil, the regular goalkeeper, was carried off injured early in the first half. "We had no backup keeper, so all the players just looked around at each other waiting for someone to volunteer. I was tall for my age, had a good reach, and thought it might be fun to try it."

He pulled on Phil's yellow top and goalkeeping gloves and took up a position between the posts. The first shot he didn't even see until it hit the back of the net. The second he managed to get his fingertips on, but he couldn't stop it crossing the line. "Come out, narrow the angle," Dave suggested. By moving off the goal line towards the player with a ball, a keeper automatically reduces the amount of the goal a striker has to aim at. "Yeah, right," Lawrence thought. "I know the theory, Davey-boy, but it's much harder than it looks."

He did improve slightly as the game progressed, made a couple of half decent saves, blocked a shot or two, and even managed to move out and narrow the angle once or twice. But, despite his height, he made a mess of collecting high crosses into the penalty area and even let a shot spin through his legs for another goal. "I don't remember if Phil was ever injured on an occasion, but if he was, I know I never volunteered to take his place again."

Goalkeepers deserve a lot of respect. It's a nerve-racking position with more responsibility and pressure than any other. A keeper needs to be determined, decisive, and brave enough to throw himself at the feet of an onrushing attacker or grab high balls in a crowded penalty area. He then needs to know exactly what he should do with the ball when he has it safely in his hands. Should he throw it out, roll it to a nearby defender, or kick it as far down the field as he can manage? If there's a defender in space (not closely guarded by an opposing player), throwing or rolling the ball to him is more accurate. If there are no defenders in space or if time is running out and his team needs a goal, kicking the ball, although less accurate, is a quicker way of getting the ball to the other end of the field.

Defenders

Defenders are the last line of defense and play directly in front of the keeper. They are responsible for stopping the opposition from having a clear shot at goal. They work to gain possession of the ball so that they can pass it to teammates to set up an attack on goal.

In a zone defense, defenders are responsible for marking, or guarding, an area of the field rather than specific players. In other words, each defender marks *any* opposing player that enters the zone the defender is responsible for. Four defenders, for example, divide the width of the field into four imaginary zones and mark one zone each.

In the zone defense, one or two center backs (also known as "center halves") play in the middle of the defense, usually with two fullbacks on either side of them—the left back and the right back.

In a man-to-man defensive system, defenders mark opposing players rather than zones. A sweeper, or *libero,* is then used in the area between the defense and the goalkeeper. He "sweeps" up any loose balls missed by the other defenders and pushes the defensive unit forward.

Defenders need to be:

1. Well-disciplined
2. Organized
3. Focused
4. Strong in the tackle

While defenders should carry the ball forward whenever they get the chance, they need to make sure there is always sufficient cover behind them in defense. In other words, if one center half, for example, runs with the ball into midfield, the other center half should stay back in case the other team wins possession of the ball and breaks quickly.

An integral part of a fullback's role is to make runs with the ball along the touch line (the "flanks") to give the team width and support the midfield and attack. But again, a fullback always needs to be aware of his defensive responsibilities and retreat quickly if the other team gains possession of the ball.

Most of the time, Lawrence played as a center back in a zonal defensive system. He was tall and strong, which helped when marking opposing center forwards, and he was quick, so it was rare for any forward to beat him to the ball. But the primary reason he chose that position was much simpler: he wanted to play every game, and there was always less competition for positions in defense than in midfield or attack.

Most kids scramble over the forward or midfield positions, the so-called glamour roles, but rarely want to play in defense. At team tryouts, he always took up a position in the forward line or on the wing, showed his speed, made a few passes, and had a few shots on goal, but when the coach asked where he liked to play, he always said, "In defense." He certainly wasn't the most skillful player, but guess what—he made every team he ever tried out for. There's much less competition for a place in defense.

Of course, it's great to score goals, rack up assists, or dribble the ball through the opposition defense, but you *do* get to do that as a defender as well on occasion, certainly more often than a forward who is stuck sitting on the bench. Good fullbacks make plenty of forward runs with the ball during a game, setting up attacks down the flanks and making crosses into the opposition's penalty area.

Many kids complain that they "don't get to do anything" as a defensive player. Of course, that's simply because some kids see glory only in scoring goals. But there's also a great deal of satisfaction to be gained from making a last-gasp tackle on a forward who is clean through on goal, or sliding in to make a goal line clearance. Kids need to be re-minded of the importance of every position. Many games are won by defenders making important tackles in the dying seconds.

Midfielders

As the name suggests, midfielders play in the middle of the field between the defense and the forwards. Often re-ferred to as the "engine room" of a team, they are usually the most hardworking players, linking defense and attack and maintaining the flow of play. When the opposition has the ball, midfield players track back to help their defenders defend. When their team has possession, midfielders sup-port their forwards in attack.

Midfielders are also usually the "creative" players on a team, players capable of creating scoring chances. Creativity is the quality that separates a good player from a great one. It's the ability to make a scoring opportunity out of nothing, to suddenly dribble past defenders, or to make an unex-pected, defense-splitting pass.

The midfield usually consists of one or two central mid-fielders playing in the middle of the field with wide play-ers—a left winger and right winger—playing outside them along the touchlines, or flanks.

Midfielders need to be:

1. Hardworking
2. Creative

3. Skillful
4. Accurate at passing

The key aspect of a role in midfield is hard work. Most games are won or lost by the team that manages to take control of the midfield, so midfield players need to work especially hard. Since it's so crucial to have a strong midfield, playing in midfield can get particularly rough. Tackles fly in; fouls are made.

John was a talented midfielder, the best on the team. He could tackle and pass well, and he always worked hard. He played alongside Heath, who, while he had some skill as a midfielder, was weak when engaged in a tackle. "Every time an opposing player tackled him, he'd dive to the ground and roll around, feigning injury," remembers John. "It broke up the rhythm of the game and frustrated his teammates as well as the opposition." A player should just pick himself up and get back on with the game.

To form an effective midfield, a coach needs to get a blend of creative and hardworking players or, ideally, players who are both.

Forwards

Forwards have the primary responsibility of leading the attack on the opposition's goal and, as the front players, or strikers, often scoring the goals. (Although, of course, any player in soccer may score a goal, regardless of position.) The forwards also assist the midfielders in shifting play from defense to attack.

Darryl was tall and strong and proved a handful for opposing defenses. While he scored a lot of goals himself, he was an unselfish player, always looking to pass the ball if a teammate was in a better position to score. Unfortunately for Danbury Boys, that teammate was usually Babs. Darryl set up chance after chance for him with neat little passes in and around the penalty area, only to see Babs scoop most of them wide or over the bar. Rather than become disheartened by his teammate's ineffectiveness in front of goal, Darryl always encouraged him and, for all his misses, Babs finished the U-10, U-11, and U-12 seasons with 20 to 30 goals against his name, most of them created by Darryl.

Forwards on a soccer team, perhaps more than any other position, depend on forming a close understanding of each other's movements to be successful. When one has the ball, for example, he can anticipate where the other will be. While some players immediately jell as a forward partnership, others only learn each other's habits and styles of play over a period of time.

Players in a flourishing striking partnership often complement each other's skills. Two players like Babs up front, for example, both set on shooting for goal rather than passing, would never be as successful as one Babs partnered with an unselfish player like Darryl. Their partnership worked because Darryl never tired of creating chances and Babs never let the misses affect his confidence.

Formations

There are 11 players per team in full-sided soccer, which AYSO recommends in the U-12 age group and above. There is always 1 goalkeeper, which leaves 10 outfield players to be distributed among the defense, midfield, and forward positions. The manner in which these 10 outfield players are distributed is known as a "formation" and is denoted by listing the number of players positioned in each area of the field. For example, one of the most commonly used formations in both professional and youth soccer is the 4-4-2 formation, which means there are 4 defenders, 4 midfielders, and 2 forwards (the goalie is not counted because every team plays with 1 goalkeeper).

It's important to remember that there's no one formation that is better than any other and there's no formation that is going to miraculously transform a losing team into a winning one. The formation selected is a matter of the coach's personal preference and the age and ability of the players. If a team is under constant pressure from the opposition or is defending a lead late in a game, for example, the coach may select to play a more defensive formation, that is, with extra defenders. On the other hand, if a team is behind and looking for an equalizing goal, the coach may opt to play with fewer defenders and more forwards.

4-4-2 Formation

The players in a 4-4-2 formation are positioned as shown on page 44.

The defenders mark any opposing striker who is positioned in their zone, or part of the field, rather than following a specific attacker into different areas of the field. The 2 center backs play little offensive soccer, often only going forward for set plays like free kicks and corners. The 2 fullbacks, however, in addition to defending, have a responsibility to carry the ball forward along the wings and support the midfielders in attack and supply crosses into the center.

The 2 central midfielders are often the creative hub of the team, distributing the ball out wide to the wingers (the left and right midfielders) and attacking through the center

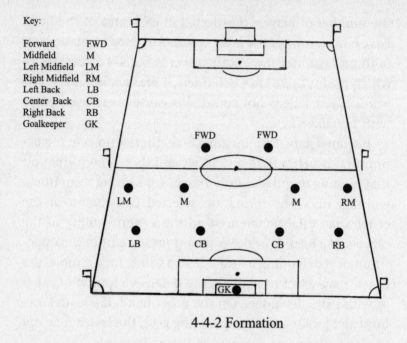

Key:

Forward   FWD
Midfield   M
Left Midfield   LM
Right Midfield   RM
Left Back   LB
Center Back   CB
Right Back   RB
Goalkeeper   GK

4-4-2 Formation

of the field. They also have a responsibility to protect their defense.

Two forwards spearhead the attack. Occasionally, 1 of the forwards might drop into a deeper position closer to the midfield to feed balls through to the other forward, or move out wide to put crosses into the box.

3-5-2 Formation

Another popular formation is the 3-5-2, which means there are 3 defenders, 5 midfielders, and 2 forwards, as shown on page 45.

The 2 central defenders operate as stoppers, marking the opposing forwards man-for-man, interchanging left and right sides as the opposing forwards interchange, as op-

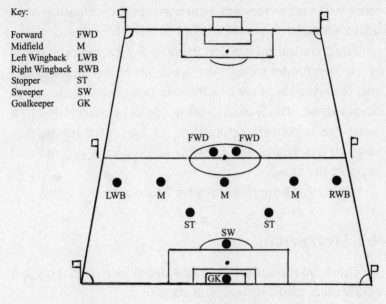

Key:

Forward	FWD
Midfield	M
Left Wingback	LWB
Right Wingback	RWB
Stopper	ST
Sweeper	SW
Goalkeeper	GK

3-5-2 Formation

posed to the flat-back four, where defenders mark the zones. The third defender acts as a sweeper, or last-chance defender. He marshals the defense, picking up any unmarked opposing midfielders who break forward, for example, or collecting any balls played by the opposition behind the defense.

The midfield in the 3-5-2 formation consists of 2 wing backs who play along the touch lines, as part wingers, part fullbacks. When the team is defending, the wing backs drop back to defend as fullbacks; when the team has the ball, they move forward in attack like wingers. Effectively, the 3-5-2 setup is a more fluid formation than the 4-4-2. When the team is defending, the wing backs drop back to change the formation from 3-5-2 to 5-3-2 (5 defenders, 3 midfielders, 2 forwards). When the team regains possession, the wing backs move forward, which makes the formation once again a 3-5-2.

The 3 central midfielders in the 3-5-2 formation have to work even harder than in the 4-4-2 formation. If, for example, the wing backs are in a forward position and the attack breaks down, the 3-man defense could be susceptible to a quick break from the opposition, so the central midfielders need to hurry back and forth to shore up the defense and support the attack.

Again, this formation calls for 2 forwards.

4-3-3 Formation

The 4-3-3 formation denotes 4 defenders in a flat back, 3 midfielders, and 3 forwards, as shown:

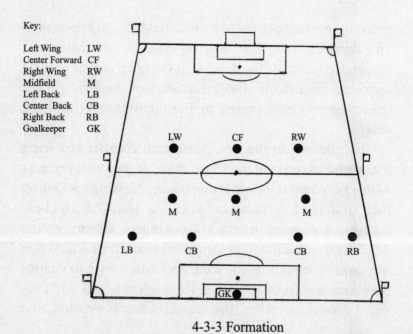

Key:

Left Wing	LW
Center Forward	CF
Right Wing	RW
Midfield	M
Left Back	LB
Center Back	CB
Right Back	RB
Goalkeeper	GK

4-3-3 Formation

The 4-3-3 usually implies that a team is willing to concede the midfield area. Since most teams play with 4 or 5 midfielders, a team playing 4-3-3 is likely to be outnumbered in midfield for most of the game. This works for a team that wants to play a more direct style of soccer. This means that instead of maintaining possession and patiently looking for gaps in the opposition defense, a team will play long balls from defense to the 3-player attack, which effectively bypasses the midfield area, where they are outnumbered.

Again, with just 3 players in midfield, the onus is on the midfielders to win the ball and play it quickly forward to their attackers rather than to patiently play it around the midfield, where they are outnumbered and more likely to lose possession.

With 3 forwards on the team, 1 usually plays in the middle as a center forward, while the other 2 move out wide to knock crosses into him.

4-5-1 Formation

The 4-5-1 lineup suggests that a team is facing superior opposition and doesn't want to concede territory in midfield or defense. Often a more defensive formation, here the burden is on the lone striker to hold the ball up while he waits for support from his midfielders. The single forward has to fight on his own for every ball played forward and works tremendously hard during a game. If this formation is played throughout an entire game, the lone forward often needs to be replaced by a substitute with fresh legs before the game is over.

Other Formations

The 5-3-2 formation adds a sweeper to a flat-back four in another defensive lineup, as does the 5-4-1, which again calls for a lone striker to hold the ball up and wait for support from his midfielders.

The important thing to remember is that formations can change throughout a game, depending on the score and the way a team is performing. A team that starts the game in a 4-4-2 formation, for example, but is a goal down late in the second half may substitute a defender or midfielder with another forward and switch the formation to 3-4-3 or 4-3-3 in the hopes of scoring.

Chapter 3

The Skills

There are several basic skills in soccer that can be learned at any age (with the exception of heading) and mastered by players who practice them regularly.

Passing

Passing is a very important soccer skill. If players do not have the ability to accurately pass the ball to teammates, the team will quickly lose possession and spend most of the game chasing after the opposition, continually trying to win back the ball.

Passing is kicking, pushing, or heading the ball to a teammate or to a space where a teammate can run on to the ball. A player may lightly tap the ball to a teammate several feet away or kick it strongly across or down the field. The ball can be played along the ground or through the air.

Most players pass the ball either using the instep of the foot for power, the outside of the boot for a short flick, or the inside of the foot to "push" the ball.

Inside-of-the-Foot Pass

The simplest, most accurate, and most frequently used form of passing is with the inside of the foot. A player places her nonkicking foot next to the ball and then strikes the ball with the flat part of the inside of her other foot, kicking the ball on the side rather than the bottom and then making sure she follows through with her kicking foot.

Outside-of-the-Foot Pass

Again, a player places her nonkicking foot next to the ball, but then she kicks the ball with the outside edge of her other foot, just below where her little toe is. As with the inside of the foot pass, a player strikes the ball at its center rather than at the bottom and swings with her lower leg. An outside-of-the-foot pass is used for a short, flicked pass. If struck with power, it will cause the ball to bend or swerve (round an opposing player or defensive wall, for example).

Making Space

Making space is an essential aspect of good passing. When a player has the ball and is looking to make a pass, it's important that her teammates move to a position where she can deliver it, a position away from a marker (member of the opposite team who might intercept it). Good players continually move around, trying to shake off the attention of a marker or draw the marker out of position in order to create space for a teammate. Players without the ball need to work just as hard as the player with the ball.

Coaches need to remind their players not to stand too

close to a teammate with the ball and make sure there isn't an opposing player between her and her teammate with the ball, which would make it easy for the pass to be intercepted.

Instinctively, young kids bunch or swarm around the ball, all following it from one end of the field to the other. As they mature, players naturally develop more awareness of their surroundings and learn to spread out across the field. Coaches can help by using practice sessions to demonstrate the value of players finding space away from the ball. Coaches can play practice games of 3 versus 2, for example, in which one team always has an extra player. If the extra player moves away from the ball, her team will find it much easier to maintain possession of the ball.

Dribbling

Dribbling is performed by maintaining control of the ball with the feet and weaving in and out of opposing players. The sight of a player using dribbling skills to beat an opponent and score a well-earned goal is one of the most exciting plays in soccer.

A player pushes the ball far enough in front of herself that she can run comfortably without the ball getting caught up under her feet, but not so far that she loses possession. Dribbling requires a combination of close control to keep the ball away from opposing players, speed to outrun pursuing opponents, and strength to shrug off any challenges. A player controls the ball with the outside of her foot (the area near the little toe) or the inside of her foot (near the big toe) or a combination of both.

Dribbling past opponents is an amazing feeling for a player and always draws cheers of excitement from spectators. But it's important that kids know not only how to dribble, but also *when* to dribble. Dribbling incurs a higher than normal risk of losing possession but, when used at the right time, can create that vital extra space for a killer pass or shot on goal. Dribbling in your own half of the field, then, runs an unnecessary risk of losing possession in a dangerous area yet offers little potential reward.

Dribbling in the opponent's half of the field, however, particularly the attacking third, offers a much greater potential reward (a shot on goal) yet has a much lower risk. Even if the ball is lost, the opposing team still has to take it to the other end of the field to make you pay for losing possession on a dribble.

Many people view dribbling as an art or talent that a player is born with, but it is a skill that can be acquired and improved upon. Players need to remember the following key points on how to beat an opponent:

1. Keep it simple—don't try to dribble the ball around every opposing player.
2. Incorporate a feint, or fake, with a change of direction to unbalance the opponent.
3. Try to cut the ball toward the back of the opponent rather than her front so she can't get a tackle in.
4. Employ a change of pace from slow or moderate during the move to an explosive burst at the end.
5. If the opponent is retreating, then attack at speed.

Ball Control

Controlling is stopping the ball with the inside or outside of the foot or allowing it to bounce off the chest, head, or thigh at an angle that deflects it to the ground to be controlled by the feet.

Controlling the Ball with the Foot

The most common way for a soccer player to control the ball during a game is by using his foot—either the inside or the outside of his foot. To control the ball with the inside of the foot, a player follows the path or flight of the ball toward him and lifts his foot even with the ball so that it hits the inside of the foot between the ankle and the toes. When the ball hits his foot, the player moves it backwards, keeping the inside of the foot touching the ball to cushion it against the ground.

Controlling the ball with the outside of the foot gives a player more time to assess his options for his next move. The outside of the foot—again, between the ankle and the toes—makes contact with the ball just as it touches the ground, making the ball immediately available for a pass or dribble.

Controlling the Ball with the Chest

A higher ball can be controlled using either the head or the chest. The chest trap is probably the second most common way of controlling the ball. The player gets in the path of the ball and pushes his chest out at it. As the ball hits his chest, he relaxes the chest to absorb the momentum of the ball and it drops to his feet.

Controlling the Ball with the Thigh

The player raises his thigh to meet the falling ball and relaxes the leg at the moment of impact, which kills the momentum of the ball and allows it to drop to the ground in front of him. With the ball under control at his feet, the player can look up and assess his options.

Heading

Heading is used to redirect or pass a ball that's too high to kick or control with the chest. It's also used effectively to score goals and defend high balls. The player times his jump so that he can climb high to the ball, and if he wants to keep the ball down, he stretches his neck to get above the ball. He then meets the ball firmly with his forehead. For a shot at goal, power is generated by a jackknife movement of the body as a player thrusts the top half of his body forward from the hips, keeping his neck muscles taut and really butting the ball hard.

The Truth about Heading

The AYSO Education Department and the AYSO Coaching Technical Committee believe that heading is an integral part of the game of soccer, and it should be introduced and taught properly to players at the appropriate age—10 years and older. Introduction to heading at an age younger than 10 or improper heading at any age may be linked to certain adverse effects.

If heading is taught correctly and executed properly by children 10 years and older, it is no more dangerous than any other aspect of youth soccer. Studies indicate that soccer is *not* the leading source of sports injuries to the head and neck, so the act of heading should be regarded within a complete context of risk. In fact, head-to-head contact among players, head contact with the ground, and head contact with goalposts and other associated playing equipment pose a greater risk than the simple act of heading the ball. These kinds of risk are associated with most outdoor team sports.

As the level of play advances and the participants' skills increase, the proper heading techniques need to be introduced to prepare the player for proper execution. Proper techniques can first be learned through the use of rag, Nerf, and inflatable balls, and an underinflated soccer ball, thus avoiding unnecessary, repetitive heading of a regulation soccer ball.

When a real soccer ball is used to practice heading, the coach should limit the length and repetitions of the drills. It's up to the coach to show the players who demonstrate a fear of the ball proper techniques so that they will not be forced to head the ball before they are ready.

Teach players to prepare to head the ball by using the following reminders:

- Keep your eye on the ball.
- Place your body so that your forehead will meet the ball.
- Take a comfortable stance with knees bent.
- Keep your eyes open and mouth closed.
- Keep your chin tucked in.
- Keep a rigid back.
- Use your arms for balance.

Coaches can teach players how to contact the ball by using the following techniques:

- Contact the ball with your forehead.
- Your legs should propel your body from the waist to head the ball.

- Your neck should be kept rigid.
- Follow through toward the target.
- Once contact is made, put your body back into a position to prepare for the next move.

Never have an unwilling player head the ball. He will not head in a game, so why force him to at practice?

One Player's Fear of Heading

Plug joined Danbury Boys at the U-12 level. In his first game, he played in the right back position and seemed to be a good all-around player, tackling hard, calling for the ball, generally immersing himself in the match. However, when it came time to defend a corner kick, it became clear that Plug had one weakness. As a right back, with the corner coming from his side, he took up a position on the near post. The ball came sailing in toward him but rather than head it clear, Plug instinctively ducked to protect his face and the ball curled into the net for a goal.

His teammates looked at him, stunned. "Don't duck, Plug," someone said to him in bemusement. "Just head it out of the way." He nodded as if he understood, and they restarted the game. A few minutes later Danbury Boys conceded another corner on the same side, and once again Plug took up a position on the near post. The ball came in and again, traveled directly toward Plug's head. At the last second, he ducked out of the way, and once more the ball sailed unchallenged into the back of the net.

It was such a comical sight to see a tall defender—he was easily the tallest player on the field—duck away from the ball that Dave and Bobby couldn't help but burst into laughter. Bobby patted Plug on the back as they walked back to take another kickoff to show him that they weren't upset with him. He told Plug that next time there was a corner, they would switch places. He would defend the near post, and Plug could mark their striker in the middle. "If you can get your chest or body in the way of the ball, great," Bobby told him. "But if not, don't worry about it." No one had any idea what caused Plug's fear of heading, but in the next two seasons that he played for Danbury Boys, none of his teammates ever saw Plug head the ball. His teammates didn't chastise him—it was clear he was nervous about heading the ball, and nobody wanted to see him do something he was uncomfortable with. So, they just accepted that Plug would never head the ball and adapted their defense accordingly.

While heading is an integral part of the game of soccer, as both an offensive and defensive technique, at youth level, as Plug proved, you can still play and enjoy the game without ever having to get your head anywhere near the ball.

Tackling

Tackling, along with intercepting a stray pass, is the most common way of gaining possession of the ball. Knowing when to tackle is as important as knowing how to tackle. A player shouldn't commit himself to a lunging, rash tackle. Using his weight to the utmost advantage, he should adopt a crouched, balanced stance and then strike hard for the ball, meeting it determinedly with the inside of his foot and forcing it away from his opponent's possession.

Tackling is not just taking the ball from the opponent, but also retaining possession of it after the tackle. Players should try to come away from the tackle having won the ball cleanly and in a position to look up field to find a team-mate who is in space and looking to receive a pass.

Shooting

Shooting is ultimately what the game of soccer boils down to. All the other skills count for little if you can't score goals. Close-range efforts can be "passed" into the back of the net using the passing techniques outlined above. However, most goals are scored by shooting hard and accurately on goal.

To combine power and accuracy, a player needs good technique. The ball should be hit firmly in the center using the top part of the foot. Like any other skill in soccer, shooting is developed through regular practice. Kids can practice in groups, each taking turns at shooting and playing keeper, or they can practice on their own, shooting the ball at a target on a wall, for instance.

The volley is a kick or shot made when the ball is still in the air before it has made contact with the ground, and is an exciting skill to master. To volley a shot on target, a player gets behind the ball and then strikes smoothly through the flight of the dropping ball, all the while remaining balanced.

Chapter 4

The Goalkeeper's Skills

Goalkeeper Control

A goalkeeper needs to dominate the area around his goal. He should call to his teammates when a ball is his, making sure that he and the defender are not both going for the same ball. He is the boss of his penalty area.

Narrowing the Angle

As a general rule, a goalkeeper should stand in the middle of the goal so he is protecting all parts of his goal equally. In other words, wherever the ball is shot—top lefthand corner, bottom righthand corner, for example—he has an equal chance of reaching the ball. By moving forward off the goal line toward the opposing player with the ball, the goalkeeper reduces the area of the goal that the player has to aim at. This is known as narrowing the angle.

If an opposing player attacks from one side, as in the diagram on the next page, the keeper moves out to make the angle so narrow that the target is reduced to the area marked

X. He covers the other areas, marked Y, so it is difficult for the attacker to put the ball past him there.

Making a Save

A basic rule for good goalkeeping is that the keeper must get his body behind the shot so that if the ball slips through his hands, his body acts as a second barrier, preventing it from flying into the net for a goal. If the shot is particularly hard, rather than catching the ball, the keeper may have to play it to the ground to take the power out of it. He should do this only if there are no forwards lurking nearby, ready to knock in an uncontrolled rebound.

Catching

Every keeper needs to have "safe hands," to be able to catch a ball cleanly, without bobbling or dropping it. To catch a ball cleanly, a keeper follows the flight of the ball and catches it with his fingers spread and his hands slightly behind the ball to stop it slipping through his hands. Again, whenever possible, a keeper should get his body behind the ball to act as a second protective barrier should the ball slip through his fingers.

Diving

A keeper dives or leaps to prevent the ball from entering the goal. Dives are made side-toward-the-ground, allowing the goalkeeper to get his body behind the ball and watch the flight of the ball as it travels toward the goal. If the ball arrives close to his body, he should attempt to catch it and pull it safely in toward his body. However, more often the keeper has to make a quick reaction dive where there is no chance of catching the ball. In that case, he should tip it safely around the goalpost or over the bar, thus conceding a corner rather than a goal.

Diving at an opponent's feet requires courage, confidence, and great skill. Coming out of goal, the goalkeeper watches the attacker's feet, waiting for him to push the ball just that fraction too far. Then he dives in to smother the ball.

Goalkeeper's Clearance

If the keeper is under great pressure from attacking players, he may be unable to cleanly catch the ball. In these instances, he should punch the ball away, using both fists if possible for more power. Once a keeper decides to go for the ball and leaves his goal line, he must be totally determined to reach the ball before anyone else. He then punches it away from danger, away from oncoming forwards. The further he punches it, the better.

Distributing the Ball

Once the ball is safely in his hands, the keeper has to distribute it to one of his outfield players within 6 seconds. He can do this by throwing or rolling the ball out to a nearby defender or by kicking the ball from the ground or drop-kicking it in a manner akin to punting a football.

Long and powerful kicks from the goalkeeper can be very useful to relieve pressure on the defense or set up a quick attack, but a quick, accurate throw to an unmarked defender in space is more likely to ensure the team keeps possession of the ball.

To kick the ball, the goalie holds it in both hands, elbows bent. As he steps forward with his nonkicking leg, he swings his kicking leg forward. He then releases the ball just before the top of his foot makes contact with it. This is a skill that's dependent on timing to ensure the ball is released at just the right moment. The more a keeper practices it, the greater his power and accuracy will become.

To throw the ball out, the keeper extends his arm with

the ball as far as possible behind his body and propels it forward in an overarm action. His arm follows through, swinging round his body for maximum power and direction. If a defender is in a position closer to the penalty area, the keeper could choose to roll or throw the ball underarm along the ground to him.

Chapter 5

The Laws of Soccer

"My mom always asks annoying questions," Jenny, the Danbury Girls keeper, used to complain. "I hate it when she tries to tells me what to do even when she doesn't know the first thing about soccer, let alone goalkeeping." She wasn't alone in her frustration. Nothing annoys kids more than parents who don't know the rules of the sport their child is playing. Fortunately for parents of soccer players, the sport your kid has chosen is remarkably easy to grasp.

Soccer is played around the world under the same set of 17 basic rules. Just think: more than 200 basic rules exist for baseball. Watch a game of professional soccer, and chances are by the end of it you'll understand as many as 15 or 16 of the 17 rules already.

The world governing body of soccer, the Fédération Internationale de Football Association (FIFA), reviews the laws of the game every year and publishes the official text of the 17 laws annually with any amendments or revised interpretations. The latest text can be found on the FIFA Web site (www.FIFA.com).

AYSO has adapted the 17 laws to account for the physical limitations of the youngest players. For the under age 12 players, the ball and the field of play are smaller, there are fewer players per team, and there are more breaks per game, otherwise the game is played exactly as FIFA laws demand.

The Laws of the Game

Law 1. The Field of Play

The soccer field is rectangular, a little larger than the size of a football field. The two sidelines, or touch lines, should be 100 to 130 yards long and are always longer than the end lines, or goal lines, which vary from 50 to 100 yards in length. All AYSO post-season playoff games are played on fields that adhere to these dimensions, although regular season games can be played on smaller fields, especially for younger teams.

The field of play is marked by 5-inch-wide lines, as shown on page 66.

1. The halfway line divides the field.
2. A circle with a radius of 10 yards surrounds the center mark, which is used to start each half and to restart the game after every goal has been scored.
3. *The penalty area:* This rectangular zone denotes the goalie's boundaries. It is only in this area that he can legally use his hands to control a ball. Any penal fouls committed by a member of the defensive team that occur in the penalty area result in a penalty kick.

    The penalty area stretches 18 yards from the inside of each goalpost and 18 yards from the goal line. The penalty arc ensures that every player

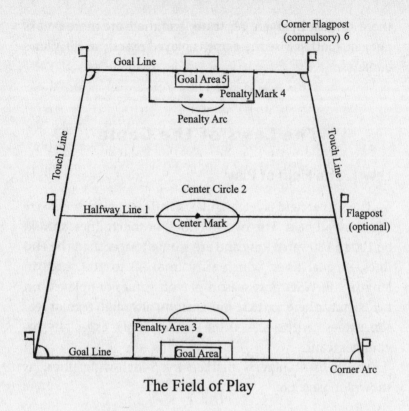

The Field of Play

(other than the goalkeeper and the kicker) is at least 10 yards from the penalty spot when a penalty is being taken.

4. The penalty spot is marked 12 yards from the midpoint of the goalposts.

5. *The goal area:* Within each penalty area is a smaller rectangle formed by two lines drawn at right angles to the goal line, 6 yards from the inside of each goalpost, called the goal area.

  The goals stand at the middle of each goal line and consist of two white upright posts 8 yards apart joined at the top by a horizontal crossbar 8 feet from the ground. Goalposts and crossbars must be made of wood, metal, or other approved material, may be square, rectangular, or elliptical, and their shape must not be dangerous to players. Nets are attached to the goals and the ground behind the goal to make it easier to see when a goal has been scored. Should the crossbar become displaced or broken during the course of a game, play is stopped until it has been repaired, or if a repair is not possible, the match is abandoned.

6. A flagpost not less than 5 feet high must be placed at each corner and may also be placed at each end of the halfway line, no closer than 1 yard to the touch line. A corner kick may be taken from anywhere inside the corner arc, a quarter circle with a radius of 1 yard from each corner flag.

Law 2. The Ball

Soccer balls have come a long way since the days when unruly mobs used to kick a pig's bladder through village streets in the Middle Ages. Today, FIFA-approved match balls are made of either leather or other suitable material and are coated in plastic to prevent water absorption in wet conditions.

Since the Middle Ages, soccer balls have been constructed of everything from rags or wicker to oranges or coconuts. Kids in South American inner cities can still be seen honing their amazing soccer skills juggling Coke cans, pieces of fruit, or ragged tennis balls. Officially, however, the soccer ball, which is round, should have a circumference of 27 to 28 inches and weigh between 14 and 16 ounces and should be replaced during a game if it bursts or becomes defective. Play is immediately stopped while the ball is replaced and then restarted by dropping the replacement ball where the ball first became defective.

Again, AYSO regulations call for smaller, lighter balls for younger age groups, is as follows:

Division	Ball Size	Circumference (inches)	Weight (ounces)
U-19, U-16, U-14	5	26.5–28	14–16
U-12, U-10	4	25–26	12–14
U-8, U-6	3	23–25	10–12

Law 3. The Number of Players

Each team has a maximum of 11 players on the field at any one time, including a goalkeeper, although AYSO games may be played with as few as 3 or 7 on each team, which allows players more touches on the ball and enables them to learn ball control, passing, and shooting skills quicker.

In official FIFA-regulated competitive matches, each team names up to 7 substitutes, of which a maximum of 3 can be used at any point during the game, either to replace injured players or for tactical adjustments. In other, non-competitive matches, more substitutes can be used if the two teams involved reach an agreement and inform the referee before the game; and in World Cup tournaments 3 substitutes can be used from 7 named.

In 11-a-side games, AYSO advocates that U-19 and U-16 age groups use a maximum of 18 players and minimum of 12 players per side and U-14 to U-8 teams consist of 12 to 15 players.

However, all divisions may opt to play with smaller teams for minisoccer, indoor soccer, or short-sided games. Skilled and less skilled players within any single age group are distributed as evenly as possible throughout all AYSO teams under the "Balanced Teams" philosophy.

In all soccer games, a substitute can enter the field of play only during a stoppage in the game, and with the referee's permission when the player being replaced has left the field.

No player or substitute shown a red card and sent off the field of play can be replaced. In such circumstances, the player's team has to play the rest of the game a player, or players, short.

As part of the AYSO "Everyone Plays" philosophy, the referee is required to stop the game midway through each half at a convenient break in play, such as a throw-in, goal kick, or a free kickoff in order for substitutions to be made. Coaches can make as many or as few substitutions at these quarter breaks or at halftime as they wish, as long as each player is on the field of play for at least half the game. Substitutions for injury can be made at any time.

Law 4. Players' Equipment

The basic compulsory equipment of a soccer player consists of a jersey or shirt, shorts, socks (still referred to as "stockings"), and appropriate footwear: cleats or sneakers with bars or studs made of nylon, rubber, aluminum, or leather, depending on the condition of the playing surface. Whatever footwear players elect to wear, the referee should inspect the studs prior to a game to ensure that they are not dangerous.

Because of the number of leg injuries incurred in soccer, players are also required to wear shin guards under their

socks at all times. Shin guards may not be the most comfortable or stylish embellishments, but neither is limping off
halfway through a game.

For all games played under the auspices of the AYSO,
players must wear the team uniform provided by the region
with the AYSO logo on the left front of the jersey and otherwise conforming to the illustration below.

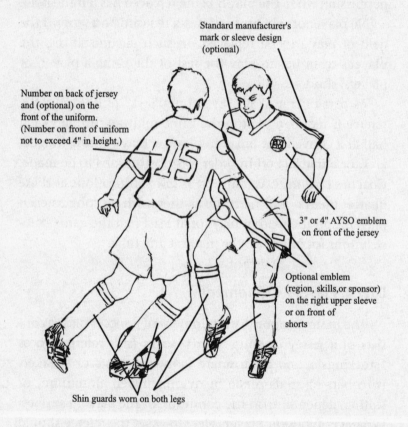

Standard manufacturer's
mark or sleeve design
(optional)

Number on back of jersey
and (optional) on the
front of the uniform.
(Number on front of uniform
not to exceed 4" in height.)

3" or 4" AYSO emblem
on front of the jersey

Optional emblem
(region, skills, or sponsor)
on the right upper sleeve
or on front of
shorts

Shin guards worn on both legs

If kids wear cycling shorts or thermal undershorts under
their shorts, these should be predominantly the same color
as the shorts. Other items of clothing, such as gloves, soft
caps without a brim, and track suit pants, can be worn with

the referee's permission. Each goalkeeper wears colors that distinguish him from both the field players and the referee. No player is allowed to wear anything that could be dangerous to himself or other players, so jewelry is removed.

Additionally, no player is allowed to take part in any AYSO training session or match wearing a cast or splint. This may sound obvious, but John can still feel the crack on the nose he received from an opposing forward during a game when the player spun round and whacked him in the face with the cast on his arm. He was told the incident resembled a slapstick sequence from a Charlie Chaplin movie, but all he saw were his hands covered in blood.

Law 5. The Referee

Each match is controlled by the referee in accordance with the laws of the game and in cooperation with two assistant referees and, where applicable, a fourth official. The referee's decisions are final, and he may change his decision only on realizing that it is incorrect or at his discretion on the advice of an assistant referee, provided that he has not already restarted play.

AYSO referees are required at all times to put great emphasis on the welfare of the players and to officiate the game in a manner encouraging clean competition and good sportmanship. In particular, it is the duty of the referee to protect the goalkeepers against dangerous play and to ensure that they are not harassed or interfered with while attempting to put the ball in play.

The referee's job is often a thankless one in soccer. His calls are sometime greeted with a torrent of protest, even abuse, from the players on the penalized team, their coaches, parents, and other supporters.

No call can ever please everyone.

A good game for a referee is often a quiet game, a game in which his presence goes unnoticed.

During a U-16 road game at the Saints, Debbie, the Danbury Girls' left back, tackled the Saints' right winger. Debbie won the ball cleanly enough, but her leg also caught the Saints player, knocking her awkwardly to the ground, so awkwardly in fact that she broke her ankle and had to be carried off the field in tears. When the game finally resumed, Saints parents and supporters shouted angrily at Debbie, obviously holding her responsible for the player's injury. Every time Debbie touched the ball, the crowd on the touch line whistled, booed, and shouted names at her. It was a horrible display and clearly upset her. She hadn't meant to hurt the Saints winger—the referee hadn't even awarded a foul against her. It was purely an accident, a regrettable but inherent risk in the game of soccer. But the spectators jeered her nonetheless, and she quickly drifted out of the game, trying her best to avoid the ball and all the unwanted attention from the spectators.

Later in the game, as Jill ran on to an angled pass into the Saints' penalty area, she stumbled and fell. To most people's amazement, the referee adjudged that a Saints defender had fouled her and blew for a penalty. The already irate home supporters couldn't believe the decision. They screamed insults at the referee, chanting the same offensive name that they had directed at Debbie earlier. The ref shook his head in disgust and then turned to Debbie. "At least they've stopped calling you that," he said.

Debbie's typically cheeky grin returned to her face for the first time since the tackle. "Yeah," she said, "but in your case it's actually true."

She was joking, of course, and fortunately, the referee did

see the funny side, but this story highlights the fruitless task that often faces a referee. A bumper sticker one AYSO ref had on his car read "Make someone happy—shake hands with a referee." It's a point worth remembering. At the youth level in AYSO, they're volunteers kindly donating their time. And like everyone else, they sometimes make mistakes. As bad as any refereeing decision may seem at the time, always remember, the game would be impossible without the men in black in the middle.

Law 6. The Assistant Referees

The two assistant referees help the referee to control the match and are directly responsible for patrolling the touch lines and indicating when the ball has passed out of the field of play; which side is entitled to a throw-in, goal kick, or corner kick; when a player should be penalized for being in an offside position (more on that later); when a substitution is requested; and when misconduct or any other incident has occured out of view of the referee.

A fourth official may be appointed to assist with substitution procedures, such as checking the replacement players' equipment, and to supervise the replacement of a damaged ball. He also has the authority to inform the referee of any irresponsible behavior by any occupant of the technical area (where coaches, managers, and substitutes watch the game).

Law 7. The Duration of the Game

The game of soccer is played in two halves, although AYSO mandates quarter breaks within each half to allow for player substitutions under the "Everyone Plays" philosophy. The duration of each half is a maximum of 45 minutes, less for younger players (see below). The half-time interval must not exceed 15 minutes.

At the end of each half, additional time is played, at the referee's discretion, to make up for time lost as a result of any substitutions, injuries, or time wasting. Extra time, or overtime, may be played according to competition rules.

AYSO rules allow for shorter halves for different age divisions, as follows:

U-19	45 minutes
U-16	40 minutes
U-14	35 minutes
U-12	30 minutes
U-10	25 minutes
U-8	20 minutes

Half-time intervals are as designated by the referee from a minimum of 5 minutes to a maximum of 10 minutes for short-sided games.

Law 8. The Start and Restart of Play

The team that wins the coin toss before the game decides which goal it will attack for the first half. The other team then gets to kick off. In the second half, the teams switch sides and the team that won the original coin toss kicks off.

The kickoff is taken from the center spot. All the players must be on their own side of the field, with the opposition standing at least 10 yeards from the ball—that is, beyond the center circle. The ball must be kicked forward and cannot be touched a second time by the kicker until another player has touched the ball. A kickoff is also taken after each goal is scored, by the team that conceded the goal, and while it is legal to score directly from the kickoff, this remains a difficult feat from that distance.

Coach Gravett came up with a typically bizarre kickoff tactic that he urged his team to employ in a game against the runaway U-15 league leaders, the Eagles. The most extraordinary thing about his master plan was that it depended on his side conceding a number of goals. Obviously, Coach Gravett had by this time relinquished all hope of the Danbury Boys ever recording a shut out.

From the first three kickoffs (the kickoff to start the game, then the next two kickoffs after the team had conceded goals) he wanted Pat to step up from defense and immediately boot the ball over the touch line as far downfield as he could manage with his powerful kick. Then on the fourth kickoff (by which time the team would have conceded three goals) he wanted Pat to again step forward. The opposing players would expect him to kick the ball out of play again, but instead Simon would dribble the ball downfield, taking them all by surprise, and score a goal. Gravett finished outlining his plan and beamed with enthusiasm.

The Danbury Boys kicked off with Pat hoofing the ball over the touch line. As Coach Gravett predicted, they did concede two early goals and at each kickoff, much to the bemusement of the opposing team, Pat again kicked the ball straight out of play. They then scored a goal themselves before conceding a third just before halftime. Coach Gravett clapped his hands enthusiastically as his players took their places for the kickoff. As planned, Pat faked to kick the ball out of play and Simon began to dribble the ball toward the opponents' goal. Rather than being taken by surprise, however, the Eagles players simply closed him down, tackled the ball from him, and began an attack of their own. Another

Gravett master stroke had once again been thwarted with incredible ease.

The only redeeming aspect of this ridiculous tactic was that a national team coach emulated it a dozen or so years later. And it was executed with similar success. This clearly reinforces what many still believe to this day. Mr. Gravett was wasted coaching youth soccer!

A dropped ball is a way of restarting the game after a temporary stoppage when the ball is still in play, such as for replacing a defective ball. The referee simply drops the ball between two opposing players at the place where play was stopped. Play restarts as soon as the ball touches the ground.

Law 9. Ball in and out of Play

The *whole* ball must cross the touch line or goal line to be out of play. The ball is in play at all other times unless stopped by the referee for a foul or any other reason. When the ball crosses either touch line, the team that last touched the ball concedes a throw-in. When the ball crosses the goal line, if the defending team touched it last, the attacking team wins a corner kick; if the attacking team touched it last, the defending team wins a goal kick.

Law 10. The Method of Scoring

Similarly, the *entire* ball must be over the goal line between the goalposts for a goal to be scored and must be in play at the time.

The team scoring the most goals during a match is the winner. If both teams score an equal number of goals, or if no goals are scored, the match is tied. Competition rules may have provisions for extra time, or overtime, a penalty

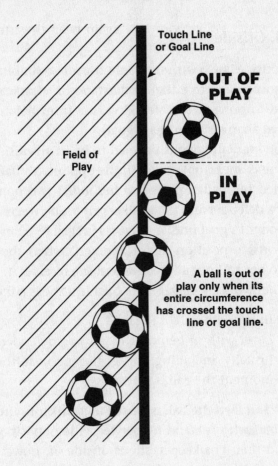

Touch Line
or Goal Line

OUT OF PLAY

Field of Play

IN PLAY

A ball is out of play only when its entire circumference has crossed the touch line or goal line.

shootout, or some other procedure approved by the International Football Association board to determine a winner.

In World Cup games, for example, teams play overtime until a goal is scored, for a maximum of 15 minutes each for two halves. If no goal is scored by the end of overtime, a penalty shootout occurs. Each team takes five penalties alternately. Whichever team scores the most penalties wins the game. If they score an equal number of these five penalties, they continue taking penalties until one team misses and the other is declared the winner.

Law 11. Offside

The offside law is without doubt the most complicated of all the soccer laws to either understand or adjudicate. It is designed to prevent the attacking side from having a flagrant goal "hanger" score easy goals.

Simply put, a player is deemed to be in an offside position if she is ahead of the ball in the opponent's half of the field when the ball is passed to her *unless* two opponents (usually a defender and the goalkeeper) are between her and the opponent's goal line. A player is judged to be in an offside or onside position at the moment when the ball is passed to her and not at the moment she receives it.

In other words, a player is *not* offside if she is either:

- In her own half of the field
- Level with or behind the last two defenders (usually including the goalkeeper), at the moment the ball is played

For example, if the ball is passed to a striker in the opposition's half who is standing between the opposition's defense and their goalkeeper, she is offside. If, however, the ball is passed forward to the striker and there are two defenders between her and the goal line, she is not offside. Similarly, if the ball is passed to the striker and at the moment at which the ball is played there are two defenders between her and the goal line, but by the time she receives the ball, the striker has run beyond that either one or both defenders, she is not offside.

In the movie *The Full Monty*, the ex-factory foreman explains how to perform a sequence of synchronized dance steps by comparing it to an offside trap in soccer. For the

OFFSIDE

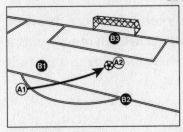

Only the Goalkeeper B3 is between Attacker A2 and the goal.

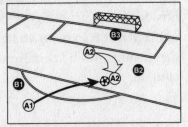

Only the Goalkeeper B3 was between Attacker A2 and the goal when the ball left A1's foot.

ON-SIDE

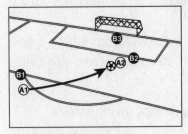

Two Defenders, B2 and Goalkeeper B3, are between Attacker A2 and the goal.

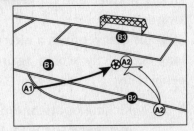

Defender B1 and Goalkeeper B3 were between A2 and the goal when ball left A1's foot.

benefit of those parents who are perhaps more familiar with cheerleading routines than soccer plays, maybe it'll help to reverse the analogy. Picture a row of five cheerleaders, four in blue outfits, one in the middle wearing red. On the drum beat, or in this case at the moment at which the ball is played forward, the four cheerleaders in blue take a step forward, leaving the cheerleader in red a pace behind. If the cheerleaders in blue are defenders and the one in red an attacker, the cheerleader in red is offside.

The referee must not penalize an offside position (and thereby keep the rhythm and entertainment of the game) if the player in that position is not involved in active play, interfering with play, interfering with an opponent, or gaining an advantage by being in that position. There can be no offside directly from a goal kick, a corner kick, or a throw-in, or if a player is in her own half of the field. In other words, a player must not be penalized merely for being in an offside *position*.

Law 12. Fouls and Misconduct

There are two types of fouls: those for which a direct free kick is awarded and those for which an indirect free kick is awarded.

Fouls that result in a direct free kick, from which a goal may be directly scored against the opponents, are called penal fouls:

- Kicking or attempting to kick an opponent, incidental to the foul
- Striking or attempting to strike an opponent
- Pushing, charging, tripping and attempting to trip, holding, or jumping at an opponent
- When tackling an opponent, making contact with the opponent before or instead of the ball
- Handling the ball deliberately (except for the goalkeeper inside his own penalty area)
- Displaying unsportsmanlike behavior, such as spitting at an opponent

A direct free kick is taken from where the offense occurred. A penalty kick is awarded if any of the above offenses is committed by a player inside his own penalty area.

An indirect free kick, which requires at least one additional player of either team to touch the ball before a goal can be scored, is awarded for nonpenal fouls:

- Dangerous play, such as high kicking near another player's head or trying to play a ball held by a goalkeeper
- Impeding an opponent (getting between him and the ball) when not playing the ball
- Impeding the goalkeeper by having excessive contact within the penalty area
- The goalkeeper taking longer than 6 seconds in possession of the ball in the penalty area or controlling the ball with his hands when the ball was last kicked to him (not headed or after it was thrown in directly to him) by a teammate

There are two kinds of misconduct, those for which a caution is awarded and those for which a player is sent off:

1. Actions that result in a caution (yellow card)
2. Actions that result in a player's being sent off or ejected from the field (a red card). A second yellow card automatically results in a red card and ejection from the game.

A player is cautioned and shown the yellow card for any of the following offenses:

- Displaying unsportsmanlike behavior
- Showing dissent by word or action
- Persistently infringing the laws of the game
- Delaying the restart of play
- Failing to respect the required distance when play is restarted with a corner kick or free kick

- Entering, re-entering, or deliberately leaving the field of play without the referee's permission
- Tackling from behind

A player is sent off and shown the red card for any of the following offenses:

- Committing serious foul play
- Exhibiting violent conduct
- Spitting at an opponent or other person
- Deliberately handling the ball to prevent a goal or an obvious goal-scoring chance for the opposition (except the goalkeeper in his own penalty area)
- Fouling an opponent who is moving toward the goal and has an obvious goal-scoring opportunity
- Using offensive, insulting, or abusive language and/or gestures
- Receiving a second booking (caution or yellow card) in the same game

Note: A tackle from behind that endangers the safety of an opponent is to be treated as a serious foul play and the player who commits this act is sent off.

While fouls, bookings, and ejections are all part of the game, they are avoidable.

Players make bad tackles, get booked, and even get sent off occasionally. It happens to everyone, right? Not exactly. England striker Gary Lineker had a long and distinguished career winning championships and cups in England, Spain, and Japan. He was awarded the Golden Boot trophy for being the top goal scorer at the 1986 World Cup Finals and was widely regarded as the best striker of his generation. And throughout his illustrious career, he was never even once cautioned, let alone shown the red card. His is a remarkable record that shows it is possible to be both the best player and the fairest.

Law 13. Free Kicks

For both direct and indirect free kicks, the ball must be stationary when the kick is taken and the kicker cannot touch the ball a second time until another player has touched it.

A goal can be scored from a direct free kick; an *indirect free kick* must be touched by a second player before it enters the goal for a goal to be awarded. If an indirect free kick is kicked directly into the opponent's goal, no goal is awarded; instead, the opposition is given a goal kick.

All opponents must be at least 10 yards from the ball when either a direct or indirect free kick is taken. If a free kick is awarded to the defending team in its own penalty area, the kick can be taken from anywhere inside the area and the opposing players must be outside the penalty area, at least 10 yards from the ball.

Free kicks awarded outside the penalty area must be taken at the place where the infringement occurred.

Law 14. Penalty Kicks

The penalty kick is awarded when a defending player commits a direct free kick foul within his own penalty area.

A player from the offended team takes the penalty kick

from the penalty mark, which is located 12 yards from the goal. All players must remain on the field outside the penalty area, and beyond the penalty mark 10 yards from the ball, until the kick is taken, except for the kicker and the goalkeeper.

The goalkeeper's feet must remain stationary on the goal line, but he may move laterally along the goal line until the ball is kicked. At the referee's signal, the kicker attempts to kick the ball into the opponent's goal and the goalkeeper tries to stop the ball from crossing the goal line.

Penalty kicks are also often used as a way of determining the winner of a tied game in certain knockout competitions, perhaps most famously demonstrated at the climax of the 1999 Women's World Cup Final.

Nothing in soccer can jangle the nerves as much as a late penalty kick or a game-deciding penalty shootout. The odds always favor the kicker, but that also means the pressure is greatest on the kicker simply because he is expected to score. The keeper is less likely to make a save, but if he does, he immediately achieves hero status.

Every season Danbury Boys had a penalty competition, partly to decide who should take the penalties awarded during a game and partly to give the goalkeeper some practice diving. Each outfield player took two sets of five penalty kicks, and the winner was the person who scored the most. John usually scored seven out of ten—okay, but by no means the best. So he's puzzled at how he came to be taking a penalty kick in the dying minutes of a tied U-14 cup game against Broomfield Lions. "I can only assume that a lot of the better penalty takers were away or out injured or just didn't want to take it," remembers John. "In any case, it was the only penalty I took during a competitive game."

He placed the ball on the penalty mark, walked to the edge of the penalty area, and then turned to face the goal. The whole game hung on this one kick. He stared at the goal. It seemed no larger than the size of a cat flap in a back door, and the goalie standing in front of it was at least 10 feet tall and 20 feet wide, and the ball he had to kick past him was bigger than a beach ball. Of course, the goalkeeper's perception of the penalty situation was probably the opposite. He probably felt like a midget in concrete boots trying to stop a rocket entering an airplane hangar.

The one thing both players have to do in a penalty situation is make a decision and stick to it. The goalkeeper has to decide which way he's going to dive. If he guesses right, there's a chance he might save the shot. The kicker has to decide where he is going to aim the ball and whether he's going to blast it with all his power or hit it softer but with more accuracy. John went for power. But the keeper guessed correctly and dived to his left. His fingertips pushed the ball against the inside of the post, but it ricocheted into the net. John sank to his knees, not in jubilation but in extreme relief. One-out-of-one. "It was a perfect penalty-taking record that I cunningly preserved by never volunteering to take another again."

Law 15. The Throw-In

When the ball has completely crossed a touch line, the team judged to have touched the ball last is penalized and a throw-in is awarded to the other team. The throw-in is taken from where the ball left the field and must be thrown with two hands from behind and over the head, while both feet are on the ground either on or outside the touch line.

Law 16. The Goal Kick

The goal kick is taken by the defending team (usually the goalkeeper) each time the ball crosses the goal line and was last touched by an attacking player. The ball may be placed anywhere in the goal area and is not considered back in play until it has been kicked out of the penalty area.

Law 17. The Corner Kick

When the ball is knocked out by the defense over its own goal line, the attacking team is awarded a corner kick. The ball is placed within the 3-foot arc in the corner of the field (nearest to where the ball went out of play) and kicked into play by the attacking team.

And that, as they say, is all there is to it. Just add excitement, a roaring crowd, and the drama of a close game, and you have a fun, rewarding, and character-building experience for players, spectators, and officials alike.

Chapter 6

Playing the Game

It's game time! This chapter provides a play-by-play guide to how a youth soccer game progresses, highlighting how to apply the rules, skills, and set plays that goalkeepers, defenders, midfielders, and strikers need to master.

When the whole team is connected and everything
is working and flowing, it's a powerful feeling.
—Mia Hamm

Mia Hamm would know much more about this than any of the Danbury Boys players, but if there was one single game that they played when everything seemed to jell it would be the U-15 playoff semifinal against Maldon Town Panthers, the team that had beaten them in the U-12 final.

Kickoff

There was a larger than usual crowd circling the field that afternoon—partly because the Panthers were such a dominant team and partly because cup games always seem to generate an extra level of excitement and interest over regular league contests.

The Danbury Boys striker, Babs, took the kickoff, tapping the ball a few inches forward from the center spot mark, and the other forward, Den, then touched it back to him. The game had begun!

Concentration

Every player in the team has to concentrate hard for the whole game, intently watching the buildup of both his own team as well as the opposition, moving off the ball to be in a position to receive a pass. The keeper needs to see when gaps appear in his defensive cover, anticipating the opponents' moves, deciding on which position he'll take up if the opposing team gains possession of the ball and makes a fast break.

Buildup Play

Creating a shooting opportunity often requires a patient buildup of the offense. In other words, a team passes the ball around, keeping possession, looking for a loose (unmarked) player who can safely receive a pass and waiting for the right moment to attack. When an early Panthers attack broke down and Phil safely gathered the ball in his hands, the Danbury Boys buildup began with his throw out to Dave, the left back, positioned near the touch line.

The emphasis throughout the buildup play was to control the ball quickly and maintain possession of it.

Goalkeeper's Throw

In this game, the tall Panthers defenders won Phil's first few high kicks down the middle of the field, so when the ball next ended up in his hands, he decided to throw it out to one of his defenders, Pat, in his own half of the field.

Phil's arm throwing the ball was extended as far as possible behind his body and he propelled it forward in an over-arm action. His arm followed through, swinging round his body for maximum power and direction.

Controlling with the Foot

As explained earlier, trapping with the foot is the most common way to control the ball. Pat moved into open space to receive the throw from Phil. His aim was to bring the ball under control quickly and safely in order to give himself maximum time to decide how to use the ball before an opponent challenged him.

His eyes and head dropped to follow the ball as it hit the ground in front of him. The outside of his foot made contact with the ball just as it touched the ground. Pat then controlled the ball, sweeping it a couple of yards up field in one fluid movement so that as his head came up to check on the position of his teammates, the ball was in front of him ready for a long or short pass or a run upfield.

Controlling the Ball with the Thigh

Another way to control the ball is with the thigh, and this is used when the ball is a few feet off the ground—too high to control with the foot but too low to control with the chest or head.

Dave collected the ball in midfield and his pass sent the ball looping through the air to Simon, a Danbury Boys midfielder, who brought the ball down with his thigh to control it quickly. He dropped the ball at his feet by raising his thigh to meet the falling ball and then relaxing and dropping his thigh at the moment of impact to kill the momentum of the ball. With the ball under control, Simon looked up to assess his options. He saw that Babs, the Danbury striker, had managed to move 3 or 4 yards away from his marking defender. Just as an opposing player slid to tackle the ball from him, Simon chipped it over his head toward Babs.

Controlling the Ball with the Chest

Balls passed high in the air are controlled by the head or the chest. In this case, as Simon's pass reached Babs in the air, Babs saw that none of his teammates was close at hand or unmarked to receive a headed pass, so he got his body in the path of the ball and pushed his chest out at it. As the ball hit him, he relaxed his chest to absorb the momentum of the ball and it dropped to his feet, safely—for the moment—out of reach of the Panthers defender coming up behind him.

Turning

Often a player receives the ball with his back toward the opposition goal. If he is closely marked by an opposing player, he can either pass the ball back the way he is facing or he can turn and try to beat the player marking him. In this instance, Babs opted for the latter. He dropped a shoulder and faked going to one side, making the defender move to cover. Babs then turned tightly with the ball to the *other* side, having created that vital space to make the turn.

Turning in tight situations, when closely marked or with fierce tackles flying in, requires courage as well as skill, but a player who has the ability to turn can create chances out of nothing and give his team scoring opportunities.

Offside

Having beaten the defender marking him, Babs looked up to pass the ball to a teammate. He saw Heath making a run toward the Panthers penalty area and sent a quick pass into his path. Heath ran onto the ball and immediately unleashed a shot—but the assistant referee's flag went up and the referee blew for offside.

At the moment Babs passed the ball, Heath had strayed beyond the last Panthers defender by a few inches. At the moment the ball was played to him, only the Panthers goalkeeper stood between him and their goal. The assistant referee made the correct decision. Heath was offside, and Panthers were awarded a free kick from the spot where Heath was caught.

Caught on the Break

Defending

The Panthers defender took the free kick very quickly, and the Panthers were suddenly launching an attack of their own. One of their forwards advanced swiftly, with the ball. One of the Danbury central defenders, Bobby, retreated toward his own penalty area, checking to see that his fellow defenders were covering other routes to goal.

Pat, playing in the other center back position, slid in for a tackle on the Panthers player, but unfortunately missed the ball completely. The attacker pushed the ball forward and skipped over Pat's legs. Now he had only Bobby to beat to get a shot on goal.

Since Bobby had no cover behind him, he tried to slow the attacking player down to give his fellow defenders time to race back behind him. He edged the attacker out toward the touch line, since few goals are scored from there. He certainly didn't want to commit himself to a hasty tackle until he had sufficient cover from the other defenders.

Once Dave and Pat were back in covering positions, Bobby moved in close to the attacker with the ball, reducing the number of attacking options and restricting the attacker's choice of making a pass to a teammate. All the while, he waited for the right moment to tackle.

Tackling

Tackling is not just taking the ball from the opponent, but also retaining possession of it. Bobby saw there was good defensive cover behind him and that the attacker was slightly off balance as he moved forward. Immediately, he moved in for the tackle. Using his weight to the utmost advantage, he adopted a crouched, balanced stance and struck hard for the ball, determined to make it his.

Bobby emerged from the tackle having won the ball cleanly and then looked up field to find a teammate in space to receive a pass.

The Counterattack

Patient probing is sometimes the only way to open up a defense; other times the quick and unexpected thrust—or counterattack—is the best route to goal.

Quick counterattacks are especially effective when a

team has been under continuous pressure for minutes on end and the opponents throw more and more players forward in an attempt to force a goal. Suddenly, one of their attacks breaks down, a defender wins the ball and spots one of his strikers lurking in space upfield. The pass is made, and perhaps for the first time in the match, the striker finds himself with the ball at his feet, open grass in front of him, and only one defender to beat before the goalkeeper.

Making Space

Making space is really about making things happen without the ball, shaking off a marker and finding space in which to safely receive a pass. As Bobby won the ball in defense, he saw his teammates upfield were all closely marked. Simon, a Danbury midfielder, suddenly made a run across the field out of his normal position. Two defenders instinctively followed him, leaving a wide-open space behind Simon that could be exploited by his teammates. Den, a Danbury forward, saw the space and ran into it, signaling to Bobby for a pass.

The Weighted Pass

It's not just the accurate direction of a pass that's important, but the *weight*—or power, intensity—of the pass as well. Without good passing, a team will not keep possession and so cannot dictate the pattern of the game.

Having spotted Den running into space at the halfway line, Bobby kicked the ball with just the right power so that it arrived in the path of Den, a few feet in front of him, so that he could run on to it without having to check the pace of his run.

Running with the Ball

Players run with the ball at their feet when there is space in front of them to do so and can then dribble or pass the ball past any approaching opponents. Den received the well-weighted pass and, with the ball at his feet, made a run for goal. Even moving at top speed, Den let his feet look after the ball while he looked up and assessed the situation in front of him. There was only one defender between him and the Panthers goalkeeper. None of Den's teammates were running in support, so there was no one to pass to. He had to go it alone.

Cutting Inside

When a player is running with the ball along the touch line in a one-on-one situation with a defender, he can either take the ball past the defender on his outside (that is, on the touch line side of the defender) or he can cut inside, away from the touch line, and head toward the goal.

Den opted for the latter. He slowed slightly, the ball at his feet on the outside of the defender, then immediately accelerated again, this time pushing the ball inside the defender. The sudden change of pace and direction completely wrong-footed the defender, and Den was left with a clear path to goal.

Den pushed the ball into the penalty area and shot. The Panthers goalie dived and just managed to get his fingertips to the ball and tip it round the goalpost and over the goal line, saving a goal but conceding a corner kick.

Corner

A high proportion of goals in soccer are scored from "set-piece" moves—plays from corners, free kicks, and long throws. Many teams practice these moves over and over so that when they occur during the course of a game, every

player on the team understands exactly what his role is. In this case, the Danbury Boys players had practiced two different corners with Simon, the midfielder, taking the kicks.

Near-Post Corner

The near-post corner is a corner kick directed toward the goalpost nearest the ball. It needs to be struck hard and fast and close to the goal. As Simon prepared to take the kick, he signaled to Babs, who was standing a few yards away from the goal. Simon crossed the ball toward the near post, and Babs sprinted the couple of yards to reach the ball with his head and direct it toward the goal.

The goalkeeper was still stranded back near the far post, with no time to get across and challenge Babs in the air. Babs made contact with the ball, sending it darting toward the goal, only to see it agonizingly bounce back off the crossbar. A Panthers defender gratefully cleared the rebound away, but the ball dropped at the edge of the area in front of Pat, who had moved up from defense to support the attack.

The Long Shot

Pat controlled the ball with one touch. Then he took a long shot on goal from about 20 yards away. He got all his weight behind the shot as he struck it; then he followed through with his foot. To keep the ball low, he made sure the knee of his striking leg was over the ball at the moment of impact. The ball whizzed through the air, beat the outstretched hand of the Panthers keeper, and rocked the back of the net. Danbury Boys were in the lead, 1–0.

The Panthers' Response

The goal seemed to galvanize the Panthers players into action, and they quickly equalized. Then they took the lead with a spectacular long-range shot that took the Danbury goalkeeper Phil completely by surprise. Danbury was 2–1 down against the best team in the league, but the team was still playing good soccer, knocking the ball around well, creating chances, and tackling hard.

Attacking Long Throw

If a player can throw the ball 30 yards or more, a throw-in taken near the opposition's corner flag can be as effective an attacking weapon as a near-post corner.

Danbury launched another attack on the Panthers defense, and one Panthers player was forced to clear the ball over the touch line, conceding a throw-in on the far-left side. Dave ran upfield to take one of his long throws that often reached into the other side's penalty area.

His throw started from way behind the touch line. Dave moved forward swiftly, stopping short of the line and releasing the ball with a strong whip-like action, his arms following through. He bent his knees and added power by thrusting his trunk forward from the hips. Both his feet remained on the ground as he released the ball.

The ball looped toward the near post. Den headed it on, but again, a Panthers defender cleared over the goal line for another corner to Danbury.

Far-Post Corner

The far-post corner is a corner directed toward the goalpost farthest from the ball. This time, Simon signaled to his teammates that the corner would be struck to sail high across the face of the goal toward the far post. Babs positioned himself on the far corner of the penalty area, and Simon launched an accurate, in-swinging cross. Babs, judging the flight of the ball, ran in and jumped to meet it with his head at the peak of his jump. Sure enough, he struck the ball perfectly and directed a bullet header beyond the Panthers goalkeeper and inside the far post. It was an excellent strike, and Danbury Boys were back on level terms, 2–2.

Goalkeeping

Once again, the goal galvanized the Panthers players, and directly from the restart, they launched a series of swift attacks. Danbury managed to clear the ball to safety the first few times, but then the burly Panthers striker got the better of Pat and was left one-on-one with Phil in the Danbury goal.

Narrowing the Angle

By moving forward off the goal line toward the opposing player with the ball, a goalkeeper narrows the angle, reducing the size of the target that the opposing player has to aim at.

Phil positioned himself perfectly to meet the Panthers striker as he cut inside from the wing. The Panthers striker shot, but because Phil had narrowed the angle so well, he was able to get his body behind the ball and make the save.

The High Catch

When an opposing player crosses the ball high in the air, a keeper will often try to catch it in the air before an opposing forward has a chance to head it toward the goal.

The Panthers winger crossed in a high ball directed toward his tall striker. In the Danbury goal, Phil judged the flight of the ball with absolute concentration and, ignoring the pressure from the opposing forwards, jumped up to grasp the ball. He formed a cradle with his hands, making sure his thumbs were at the back of the ball, and pulled it down into his body as he dropped to the ground. It was a clean catch.

Goalkeeper's Clearance

If the keeper is unable to cleanly catch the ball, as in the example above, he should punch the ball away, using both fists if possible for maximum power and distance.

When a Danbury defender knocked the ball over his own goal line, the ref awarded the Panthers a corner kick. The high corner sailed across the face of the goal just outside the goal area. The attacking players and his own defenders had Phil hemmed in. He knew he wouldn't be able to catch the ball cleanly, so he decided to punch the high ball away, using his fists. He launched himself at the ball and punched it hard with two clenched fists, clearing it as far away from the goal as possible.

The Goal Kick

A goal kick is taken by the defending team when the ball has crossed the goal line and was last touched by an attacking player. When Phil punched the ball out of the danger zone, a Panther took a wild shot, sending the ball harmlessly over the Danbury goal line for a goal kick. Phil never took the goal kicks himself, since he didn't have a very powerful kick. Usually, that responsibility fell to one of his defenders.

On this occasion, Pat placed the ball at the edge of the goal area, waited for the last player to get out of the penalty area, then launched the ball into the midfield area to set up another Danbury Boys attack.

Midfield Play

Midfield players are often referred to as the "engine" room of the team, and the midfield is where most matches are won or lost. Possession of the ball is vital. The team with the ball is the team that can attack. The team in possession dictates the play. The midfield is the area where the defense must become organized—where pressure and close marking break up the opponents' attack. But the midfield is also the springboard for attack, the area where pressure is built up on the opponent's defense.

Interception

Winning possession of the ball is a key skill of the midfield player. Simon watched the ball as the Panthers worked it patiently out of defense. Reading the play and guessing his opponents' next move, Simon quickly moved to intercept a pass as their attack moved into the Danbury half of the field.

The midfielder needs strength, speed, and determination to win what, in soccer, is called a 50-50 ball—that is, a ball that both opposing players have an equal chance of winning.

The Short Pass

The short pass of just a few yards is a safe and sure way of building an attack. The shorter the distance a ball has to travel, the less chance there is of an interception. Once he had intercepted the ball, Simon looked to play it off to a nearby teammate. There are many ways of kicking a short pass—this time Simon used a quick stub with his instep, the toe pointed down. Alternatively, he could have pushed the ball with the inside of his foot to ensure greater accuracy.

As a midfielder, Simon was always looking for the pass that not only maintained possession but also took a defender out of the game, giving his teammate who received the ball unchallenged progress forward.

The Long Pass

The long pass is a faster way to build an attack, sending the ball from one end of the field to the other. But because of the greater distance the ball has to travel, there is more chance that an opponent will intercept it. Simon had the vision and confidence to hit a long pass out of his own half, sending the ball upfield to Babs, the striker. The accomplished midfield player needs to be able to keep a constant check on where everybody is on the field, so that as he gains possession of the ball he can quickly make his choice of the best pass available.

Simon hit the ball hard and true with a long follow-through of his leg. It was the type of pass that would keep on moving after bouncing, so Babs had to break into a sprint to run onto it before it went over the touch line and out of bounds.

Bending the Ball

Bending the ball is a way of passing or shooting the ball so that it swerves or bends in mid-flight. This is often referred to as a "banana" shot or pass since the trajectory of the ball follows the shape of a banana; that is, it curls out, then back in. A player bends the ball by hitting it with a glancing blow on one side.

Dave dribbled the ball out of defense along the left touch line. But when he saw a Panthers defender blocking his advance down that side, he switched play to the other side of the field. He did this by bending the ball around the Panthers defense, to Simon on the other wing.

Swift changes in the point and direction of an attack unsettle the opposing defense. The Panthers defenders shifted their attention to the new threat—loosening their marking on the Danbury strikers for a brief but vital moment.

Shielding the Ball

A player "shields" ("screens") the ball by keeping his body between the ball and the opposing player, so that the other player can reach it only by fouling him. Keeping the ball is vital. Only the team with the ball can build attacks and score goals. A selfish player who runs into trouble with the ball may make a bad pass to a teammate who has no chance of keeping possession.

Heath screened, or shielded, the ball from an opponent only for a second or two, but long enough for Den to run into a position where Heath could pass the ball to him safely.

The Short Throw

The short throw is directed toward a teammate close to the part of the touch line where the throw is being taken. The short throw often requires the thrower's teammates to keep changing position until space is made for a throw to ensure that the team keeps possession of the ball. If the player about to receive the ball is closely marked from behind by an opponent, a good move is often to fake a run upfield and then—as the marking opponent begins to follow—to stop dead so that there's a brief moment unmarked.

When a Panther knocked the ball over the touch line for a throw-in to Danbury, Heath ran over to take a short throw. Heath had his hands at the back of the ball, which gave him control and power. His feet were firmly planted behind the touch line, and of course, to make the throw legal, he made sure the ball went behind his head before he threw it. Then, he threw the ball quickly, knee high, to the right back, Plug; Plug then volleyed it straight back to him with the inside of his foot so that Heath ended up with the ball back at his feet and space in which to consider what to do next.

Changing Pace

A good midfield player controls the speed of the game to suit his own teammates. If they are under pressure and rushed off their feet, he attempts to slow the pace down to give them time to catch their breath and regain their confidence. If there's a sudden gap upfield in the opponent's defense, he may swing a quick hard pass into the space to allow one of his attackers to rush onto the ball and shoot at goal.

Simon brought the ball forward into the Panthers' half of the field at little more than walking pace. Sensing the opposing defense had been lulled into a false sense of security, he suddenly exploded forward into a dash toward the goal, bursting past the first defender in front of him, who was left rooted to the spot by the abruptness of his move. Immediately, the opposing defense was thrown into panic, with nobody quite sure whether to come across to tackle Simon in case he tried a shot at goal or whether to carry on marking his teammates, Babs and Den.

Free Kick

A free kick is the start of a potential scoring situation. Cool thinking is even more important than quick action. Understanding between players is key.

Swerving Shot

A swerving, or banana, shot, like a swerving pass, causes the ball to bend in mid-flight. Danbury was awarded a direct free kick just outside the Panthers' penalty area. The Panthers defenders quickly formed a defensive wall to block one side of the goal while the goalkeeper guarded the other side.

Both Den and Simon stepped up to take the kick. It was a play they had rehearsed in training on several occasions. Den ran over the ball to confuse the opposition defense, and Simon went for a direct shot by curving the ball round one end of the wall and into the top lefthand angle of the goal. He struck the ball with the inside of his right foot so that the ball swerved in flight.

Some players are so good at these swerving free kicks round the end of the wall, that defenses often arrange the wall so that it stretches a foot or two outside the far goalpost as well as the goal itself, to cut off even the sharpest swerve. But in this case, Simon's shot was good enough to beat the wall and the goalkeeper: 3–2 Danbury Boys!

The Chip Pass

A chip pass is used to hook, or chip, the ball *over* an opposing player as opposed to *around* him.

When Danbury was awarded a second free kick just outside the Panthers' penalty area, Simon chipped the ball over the defenders' heads toward Babs, who had moved into position to receive the pass.

Simon made the ball drop into the area by getting his toe under the ball and stopping his foot dead as it struck the ball sharply.

The Volley

A volley is a shot or pass struck while the ball is still in the air, before it has hit the ground. There is nothing quite as exciting as watching a player shoot a ball on the volley.

As Simon chipped the ball over the defensive wall, Babs timed his run perfectly. Before he could be challenged, Babs moved his feet quickly to get behind the ball. Then he struck smoothly through the flight of the dropping ball, all the while perfectly balanced. The result was power and accuracy as he cracked the ball on the volley. It spun toward the righthand corner in an unstoppable shot. Danbury was now 4–2 ahead!

The Restart

The Panthers, having conceded the goal, kicked off again from the center spot, in just the same way Danbury had to start the game.

Playing the Advantage Rule

The advantage rule enables the ref to overlook a foul or infringement if the team that's been fouled already has possession of the ball. For example, when Dave tried to intercept a pass from one Panthers player to another, the ball struck his hand and the Panthers supporters on the touch line immediately shouted for a free kick. The referee, however, saw that the ball had bounced from Dave's hand into the path of an advancing Panthers player. Rather than whistle to stop the play, he invoked the advantage rule, signaling with both arms out that play should continue since the Panthers already had possession of the ball in a good position on the field.

Stopping the play at this point would have punished the Panthers more than Danbury and would also have broken up the flow of the game. Had Dave and the Danbury Boys gained an advantage from his illegal use of his hand, the referee would instead have blown for a free kick to the Panthers.

Yellow Card

With Danbury caught on the break, Plug, the right back, found himself outnumbered in defense against the Panthers attackers. The Panthers striker dribbled past him, and Plug made the mistake of lunging in with a rash challenge from behind the player. Plug missed the ball but caught the Panthers striker's legs, upending him just outside the Danbury penalty area.

The referee immediately blew for a free kick. Plug apologized to the Panthers player and helped him back up to his feet. There was no malicious intent in the tackle—it was just badly timed. However, tackling from behind can be dangerous, and under today's rules, any player who fouls in that manner will be cautioned and shown the yellow card or immediately sent off if the fouled player was clean through on goal.

The referee took Plug's name and raised the yellow card above his head. If Plug committed another serious foul, he would be sent off, leaving Danbury Boys a player short.

Defending the Free Kick

The Panthers now had a chance to threaten the Danbury goal with a free kick. Phil, the Danbury keeper, took responsibility for organizing the defensive wall in front of him.

The Defensive Wall

The object of the wall is to deny the opposition a direct shot at goal from a free kick. The wall should cover one part of the goal while the goalkeeper covers the rest.

Here, an opponent took up a position at the edge of the Danbury defensive wall, to confuse the defenders. He could move suddenly and create a gap for the free kick taker to strike the ball through.

In this instance, however, rather than strike directly for goal, the Panthers player simply kicked the ball diagonally across the goal for another Panther to run onto for a clear shot at goal, thus defeating the object of the wall with just one short pass.

Saving a Hard Shot

The Panthers attacker ran onto his teammate's pass and fired off a fierce shot at the Danbury goal. Phil, the keeper had his work cut out trying to stop it from hitting the back of the net. He moved quickly to get his body behind the shot, so that if the ball slipped through his hands, at least his body would prevent it from going into the net.

Phil crouched to form a hollow between his chest and arms to cradle the speeding ball. On contact, his hands folded up behind the ball, closing the perfect trap.

Defensive Header

The defensive header is employed by defenders to clear high crosses and corners from the danger area near their goal. The Panthers continued to pressure the Danbury goal, but they defended their lead resolutely. Even the forwards dropped back to help win the ball. When the Panthers winger crossed the ball in toward their center forward, Pat moved across to clear the ball as it floated high across his penalty area. By standing just a few yards off the attacker he was marking, Pat gave himself the room to run three or four paces before jumping for the ball. This gave him an extra thrust off the ground so he could gain more height in his jump. His aim was to reach the ball before any of the Panthers attackers, and to get plenty of distance with his headed clearance by hitting the underside of the ball with his forehead.

When under strong pressure from the Panthers strikers, both center backs—Pat and Bobby—deliberately headed the ball over the touch line for safety; it's much better to concede a throw-in than a goal. If they had more time, they would attempt to direct their headers to one of their teammates further upfield. But whatever they decided to do, they always wanted to avoid heading the ball to a Panthers player on the edge of the penalty area, which would give the Panthers a great shooting opportunity.

Second Half

There was no more scoring before the halftime interval. The Panthers attacked right from the second half kickoff, and the Danbury players were all a little slow to react. By the time they were midway through the second half, the Panthers had fought their way back into the game and taken the lead at 5–4. The Danbury Boys players knew that to win, they would have to use all their offensive tricks and skills.

The One-Two Pass

The one-two pass is also called a wall pass: one player passes the ball to a teammate who acts as a wall by immediately returning the ball to him. Bobby ran with the ball at his feet and skipped past a couple of tackles. He reached the edge of the Panther's penalty area, which was tightly packed with defenders determined to keep out the attack.

As Bobby approached the penalty area, he used a quick one-two pass with Dave. Bobby ran at the goal, and as another Panthers defender moved out to challenge him, he pushed the ball to Dave and kept running. The defender hesitated. Dave pushed the ball straight back into Bobby's path as he continued moving forward. The defender was out of the play without having had the chance to tackle.

Dummying

Dummying is feinting, or faking, a move to confuse or wrong-foot the opposition. With the ball back at his feet, Bobby looked up to see Simon dart inside the penalty area. Bobby immediately crossed the ball toward him. The tall Panthers defender saw Simon about to take the ball in his stride and began to move to cut off Simon's route to goal. But Simon cleverly faked the play: instead of pushing the ball forward, he stepped over it, allowing Bobby's pass from the wing to go straight through to Babs behind him. In the split second that the Panthers defenders and goalkeeper were still poised to meet the drive from Simon, Babs shot for goal and the ball rocketed into the back of the net. Danbury was level again, 5–5, and Babs had scored a hat trick (three goals in a single game).

Quick Reactions

When the ball comes to a player in a tightly packed penalty area a few yards from his opponent's goal, his only objective is to kick, head, or somehow scramble it quickly into the back of the net. Elegant methods are not necessarily the best. Many a good goal has been scored from short range off a striker's knee, shin, chest, or even the back of his head. In these situations it's instant reactions that count—getting to the ball first and stabbing it into the net any legal way.

Danbury Boys broke quickly from defense, and Dave crossed the ball hard into the Panthers' penalty area. It bobbled around between players before finally breaking loose. Den rushed in headlong from the edge of the penalty area to meet the ball. It was too high to volley and too far ahead of him to control with his chest, so he simply launched himself at the ball in a flying dive, using all the forward momentum of his run, and thumped the ball into the net using the flat of his forehead. It wasn't the prettiest goal ever seen, but it was one of the most welcome. Danbury was now ahead 6–5, with only a few minutes left on the clock.

The game really opened up now. With the minutes ticking away, the Panthers players sensed they were in real danger of losing the game and being knocked out of the cup. They threw players forward, attacking in numbers in a desperate attempt to snatch an equalizer. But Danbury defended stoically.

The Back Heel

Attacking players often receive the ball with their backs to goal, and in a tightly packed penalty area, they don't always have the time to turn with the ball to shoot or pass. In these situations, they can back-heel the ball, passing or shooting it using their heel.

The Panthers midfielders moved up into attack to help the Panthers convert their strong pressure into a goal. The Panthers center forward stabbed the ball to his captain quickly along the ground. Pat was upon him immediately, though, and then Dave and Bobby arrived to lend support and crowd in on the player with the ball.

With no time to turn, however, the Panthers captain cleverly back-heeled the ball toward the Danbury goal and into the path of his onrushing striker. It was an unexpected move that took the Danbury defense by surprise and earned the Panthers another shot at goal. The striker fired in a hooked shot that looped over the Danbury keeper, Phil, and across the goal line. From nowhere, the right back, Plug, jumped in to head the ball away just as it was about to cross the line.

The referee quickly consulted with the assistant referee, who had a side view of the goal line. He told the ref that the *entire* ball had not crossed the line, so the ref waved away the protests of the Panthers players and signaled that no goal has been scored. Danbury Boys were still ahead 6–5.

Penalty

The referee awards a penalty to the attacking team when a member of the defending team commits a foul inside his own penalty area. The penalty is one of the most dramatic of all soccer moments of truth, especially when it occurs near the end of a close game. Two players face one another, pitting their skills and knowledge against one another to make or prevent a goal. The odds, however, are always against the goalkeeper.

Penalty Kick

In typically dramatic fashion, it was the last minute of the game when the Panthers were awarded a penalty after Plug had illegally handled the ball in his penalty area. It was a harsh decision by the ref. Plug and his teammates felt that the handling was accidental—the ball had hit his arm rather than the other way around. But the referee judged it a deliberate hand ball and awarded the Panthers a penalty. There was no point in the Danbury players arguing.

The Panthers captain placed the ball on the Danbury penalty spot, which is located 12 yards from the center of the goal line. The Danbury keeper, Phil, stood on his goal line and took a deep breath. The whole game was now hanging on this one kick of the ball. Every other player stood outside the penalty area, waiting for the ball to be struck.

The Panthers captain knew exactly where he intended to place the kick before he stepped up to the ball. He had a deceptive run leading up to the ball that was meant to send Phil diving the wrong way. By keeping the knee of his kicking leg well over the ball to keep the kick low, he struck the ball firmly, low and hard toward the corner of the goal.

Diving

Many goalkeepers commit themselves to diving to one side of the goal in order to at least give themselves a 50–50 chance of going the right direction, and if the ball has been even slightly misdirected or if it has not been hit with enough power, they may be able to reach it.

Other Panthers players moved in from the edge of the penalty area as soon as their captain kicked the ball, in case Phil parried the ball. This would give one of them the opportunity to score from the rebound.

But Phil dived side-toward-the-ground when the ball was struck, which allowed him to get his body behind the ball and watch the flight of the ball as it traveled toward the goal. If the ball arrived close to his body, he would attempt to catch it and pull it safely in toward his body. But the ball was heading toward the corner of the goal. Phil stretched and just managed to get his fingertips to the ball, tipping it safely around the post.

The Danbury Boys all jumped up and down, wild with

excitement. They had won the game by the narrowest of margins and went on to the cup final. Just as important, they had all put in maximum effort and had enjoyed every single kick of the game.

> *After each game, I want to be able to say:*
> *I gave it all that I should. I gave it my best.*
>
> —Mia Hamm

Chapter 7

Short-Sided Soccer

Why Short-Sided Soccer?

Short-sided soccer is the most appropriate introduction to the game for boys and girls under 12 who want to play soccer but aren't ready to cope with the demands of a full 11-a-side game. Short-sided games are played with reduced team numbers (3 to 9 players), smaller-sized fields, shorter playing times, and smaller balls, which are much easier for children to control and therefore help build confidence in the players.

The use of fewer players on a smaller playing area ensures that players participate more in the game, which in turn helps them develop skills and techniques faster. More touches of the ball means more fun and more opportunities for improving play and learning the game. The more individual success children experience on the soccer field, the more self-esteem they develop off it and the more likely they are to want to return for the next season.

Children under 12 relate more readily to smaller groups of players. They also have a limited attention span, which precludes prolonged periods of activity. Most important, children focus best when learning activities are fun. Short-

sided soccer is always fun and interesting because the players are always in the vicinity of the ball. They cannot "hide"
in a game or have the unfortunate experience of the ball
rarely appearing in their part of the field. In an 11-a-side
game with young players on a full-sized field, it's possible
for a player to kick the ball only a few times in a game.

The rules for AYSO short-sided games are less stringent,
as a way to ease both players and parents into an understanding of the game and to ensure that games flow. For example, there are no offsides and no yellow or red cards
shown to the youngest players. Rather, referees are encouraged to take the time to explain to a player why his actions
violated the rules. For AYSO players, short-sided soccer is all
about team spirit, skills development, and, of course, enjoyment.

Short-Sided Soccer *Is* Real Soccer

The richly talented Brazilians have long dominated world
soccer and have given the game players of the caliber of Pelé,
Zico, Juninho, Romário, Rivaldo, and Ronaldo. These players, along with most Brazilian children, honed their amazing skills by playing short-sided soccer. In Brazil, it's called
futebol de salão (hall soccer) and is played on a field the size of
a basketball court with a size 2 ball and 5 players to a team.
The game is credited as being the largest single factor in pro-
ducing so many of the world's most skillful players. Ronaldo,
World Player of the Year in 1997 and 1998, played this short-
sided game until 1994, when he was 17.

Short-sided soccer is one of the best ways to develop a
youngster's ball control, passing, and dribbling—the skills
for which the Brazilians are best known. The smaller fields

also encourage the players to move without the ball in order to create free space in which to receive a pass from a team-mate—an important technique when playing conventional 11-a-side soccer.

As well as easing children into the game of soccer, short-sided games are also an ideal way to ease adults into coaching and refereeing. Since almost 70 percent of AYSO coaches are parents with no prior exposure to soccer, the simplified rules, reduced number of players, and smaller playing area make it easier for first-timers to gain a better understanding of soccer.

U-6 Short-Sided Rules

Play in this very young age group is meant to give a taste of the game, some experience in working together as a team, and most of all, a positive introduction to the soccer experience.

One of the most appealing things about soccer as a youth sport is that practically no skills at all are required to play the game at its simplest level. If a youngster can run and can kick a ball, he or she can play and enjoy soccer.

1. The Field of Play

The playing area should be a maximum of 30 yards long and 15 yards wide, about the size of a basketball court. Distinctive lines are not required; the field can be marked using cones. The goals should be no larger than 4 feet high and 6 feet wide.

Spectators are not allowed behind either goal or within 3 yards of either touch line. Parents and players can encourage players, but not coach or instruct them, during the course of the game.

2. The Ball

A size 3 ball should be used, 23 to 25 inches in circumference, 10 to 12 ounces in weight.

3. The Number of Players

AYSO does not endorse coed teams. Separate boys' and girls' teams are promoted at all levels. Each team has a maximum of 5 players on the roster, with no more than 3 players on the field at any one time (and no goalkeeper). As part of the "Everyone Plays" philosophy, each child on the roster plays a minimum of 50 percent of the playing time, 75 percent whenever possible. Substitutions can be made at halftime or when the referee stops the game midway through each half. Substitutions for injury can be made at any time.

4. Player's Equipment

Appropriate footwear for this age group means regular sneakers or soft-cleated soccer shoes. Shin guards are mandatory for practices as well as games. No player is allowed to take part in practice or a game wearing a cast or splint.

5. Referees

The referee can be either a registered referee, a youth referee, a coach, or a parent (any registered AYSO volunteer) and should always emphasize safety, fairness, fun, and learning. AYSO referees are encouraged to explain any infringements to the player or players and assist in familiarizing players with the game.

6. Assistant Referees

No assistant referees are required at the U-6 level.

7. Duration of the Game

U-6 short-sided games are played in halves of 10 minutes each, with quarter breaks within each half to allow for player substitutions—that is, breaks every 5 minutes. Halftime intervals are as designated by the referee, from a minimum of 5 minutes to a maximum of 10 minutes.

8. Start and Restart of Play

The coaches determine which team starts the game, and the opposing team starts the second half.

Instead of a kickoff, the U-6 short-sided game is started with a free kick taken from the middle of the field. The opposition players must be at least 5 yards from the ball when the kick is taken.

After each goal is scored, the team that conceded the goal takes a similar free kick from the middle of the field rather than a goal kick because the field of play is so small.

9. Ball in and out of Play

The *whole* ball must cross the touch line or goal line to be out of play. The ball is in play at all other times unless the game is stopped by the referee for a foul or any other reason.

10. Method of Scoring

As in conventional games, the *entire* ball must be over the goal line between the goalposts for a goal to be scored.

At the U-6 level, games are noncompetitive, so game scores and league standings are not recorded. All players should receive participation awards.

11. Offside

There is no offside law in AYSO U-6 short-sided soccer.

12. Fouls and Misconduct

All fouls result in a direct free kick, with the opposing players required to be at least 5 yards from the ball when the kick is taken. There are no yellow card cautions or red card dismissals at this level. The referee should simply explain to the player or players involved why a certain action is not permitted and award a free kick.

13. Free Kicks

All free kicks are direct free kicks (can be kicked directly into the opponent's goal). The ball must be stationary when the kick is taken, and the kicker cannot touch the ball a second time until another player has touched it.

14. Penalty Kicks

There are no penalty areas at the U-6 level; therefore, no penalty kicks can be awarded.

15. Throw-In

As under the regular laws, when the ball has completely crossed the touch line—either on the ground or in the air—a throw-in is awarded against the team that last touched the ball.

The throw-in is taken from where the ball left the field and must be thrown with two hands from behind and over the head, while both feet are on the ground behind the touch line. However, at this age, referees should not penalize players for failing to make a technically perfect throw.

16. Goal Kicks

There are no goal kicks at this level. When the whole of the ball is kicked over the goal line (not into the goal) by an attacker, it is kicked into play from where it crossed the line by a member of the defending team.

17. Corner Kicks

Likewise, there are no corner kicks at this level. Again, when the whole of the ball is passed over the goal line (not into the goal) by a defender, it is kicked into play from where it crossed the line by a player on the attacking team.

U-8 Short-Sided Rules

New and exciting adventures begin to open up to the U-8 players as their coordination improves and their size and strength increase. However, new challenges are often met with a mixture of enthusiasm and frustration. U-8 players typically set unrealistically high standards for themselves, have difficulty making choices, and at times are over-whelmed by unfamiliar situations. They are at the awkward phase where they know enough to understand the complexities of the game, but still have much to learn about implementing their knowledge.

1. The Field of Play

The playing area should be a maximum of 50 yards long and 25 yards wide, about half the size of a regular field. Distinctive line markings are recommended over cones.

The field is divided in half by a halfway line, and a center circle with a radius of 6 yards is marked from the midpoint of the halfway line.

The goal area in front of each goal measures 6 yards by 12 yards, and the corner arc at each corner of the field is marked with a 1-yard radius.

The goals should be a maximum of 6 feet high and 6 yards wide.

Spectators are not allowed behind either goal or within 3 yards of either touch line. Parents and players can encourage players, but not coach or instruct them, during the course of the game.

2. The Ball

A size 3 ball should be used, 23 to 25 inches in circumference, 10 to 12 ounces in weight.

3. The Number of Players

Each team has a maximum of 8 players on the roster, with up to 5 players, including a goalie, on the field at any one time. Each player on the roster plays a minimum of 50 percent of the playing time, 75 percent if possible.

Substitutions can be made at halftime or when the referee stops the game midway through each half. Substitutions for injury can be made at any time.

4. Players' Equipment

Appropriate footwear for this age group means sneakers or soft-cleated soccer boots. Shin guards are mandatory for practices as well as games. No player is allowed to take part in practice or a match wearing a cast or splint.

5. Referees

The referee should be a registered AYSO volunteer—either a registered referee, a youth referee, or a coach—and should always emphasize safety, fairness, fun, and learning. AYSO referees are encouraged to explain any infringements to the player or players and assist in familiarizing players with the game.

The decision of the referee is final and must not be questioned by coaches. A referee may only change his decision on realizing that it is incorrect or, at his discretion, on the advice of an assistant referee, provided that he has not already restarted play.

6. Assistant Referees

Parents may be used as assistant referees to help the referee in controlling the game in accordance with the laws of the game.

7. Duration of the Game

U-8 short-sided games are played in halves of 20 minutes each, with quarter breaks within each half to allow for player substitutions. Halftime intervals are as designated by the referee, from a minimum of 5 minutes to a maximum of 10 minutes.

8. Start and Restart of Play

There is no change from regular play, except that opposing players must be 6 yards from the ball when the kickoff is taken.

9. Ball in and out of Play

As in regular play, the *whole* ball must cross the touch line or goal line to be out of play.

10. Method of Scoring

Again, there is no change from conventional play: the *entire* ball must be over the goal line between the goalposts for a goal to be scored.

As at the U-6 level, U-8 games are noncompetitive, so game scores and league standings are not recorded. All players should receive participation awards.

11. Offside

There is no offside law in AYSO U-8 short-sided soccer.

12. Fouls and Misconduct

All fouls result in a direct free kick, with the opposing players required to be at least 6 yards from the ball when the kick is taken. Referees work cooperatively with coaches to eliminate the need for yellow card cautions or red card dismissals.

All infractions should be explained to the player or players involved.

13. Free Kicks

All free kicks are direct free kicks (can be kicked directly into the opponent's goal). The ball must be stationary when the kick is taken, and the kicker cannot touch the ball a second time until another player has touched it.

14. Penalty Kicks

There are no penalty kicks at U-8 level. Free kicks awarded to the attacking team inside the goal area should be taken from the nearest point on the goal area line in front of the goal.

15. Throw-In

As under the regular laws, when the ball has completely crossed the touch line—either on the ground or in the air— a throw-in is awarded against the team that last touched the ball.

The throw-in is taken from where the ball left the field and must be thrown with two hands from behind and over the head, while both feet are on the ground behind the touchline. A second throw-in is allowed if a player commits a foul on the initial attempt. The referee should explain the proper method before allowing the player to throw again.

16. Goal Kicks

The goal kick is taken by the defending team each time the ball crosses the goal line and was last touched by an attacking player. The ball may be placed anywhere in the goal area, and opponents must be 8 yards from the ball when the kick is taken.

17. Corner Kicks

No change from regular play (the corner kick is taken by the attacking team each time the ball is knocked out by the defense over its own goal line) except that opponents must be at least 8 yards from the ball when the kick is taken.

U-10 Short-Sided Rules

1. The Field of Play

The playing area should be a maximum of 80 yards long and 40 yards wide. The field is divided in half by a halfway line, and a center circle with a radius of 8 yards is marked from the midpoint of the halfway line.

The penalty area stretches 14 yards from the inside of each goalpost and 14 yards from the goal line. Within each penalty area is a smaller rectangle formed by two lines drawn at right angles to the goal line, 6 yards from the inside of each goalpost, called the goal area. The penalty spot is marked 10 yards from the center of the goal line, extending from which is the penalty arc at an 8-yard radius.

A corner arc with a 1-yard radius is marked at each corner of the field.

The goals should be a maximum of 6 feet high and 6 yards wide.

Spectators are not allowed behind either goal or within 3 yards of either touch line. Parents and players can encourage players, but not coach or instruct them, during the course of the game.

2. The Ball

A size 4 ball should be used, 25 to 26 inches in circumference, 12 to 14 ounces in weight.

3. The Number of Players

Each team has a maximum of 10 players on the roster and can play up to 7 at any time, 1 of whom may be a goalkeeper. Each player on the roster plays a minimum of 50 percent of the playing time, 75 percent if possible.

Substitutions can be made at halftime or when the referee stops the game midway through each half. Substitutions for injury can be made at any time.

4. Players' Equipment

Appropriate footwear for this age group means sneakers or soft-cleated soccer boots. Shin guards are mandatory for practices as well as games. No player is allowed to take part in practice or a match wearing a cast or splint.

5. Referees

The referee should be either a registered referee or a youth referee and should always emphasize safety, fairness, fun, and learning. AYSO referees are encouraged to explain any infringements to the player or players and assist in familiarizing players with the game.

The decision of the referee is final and must not be questioned by coaches. A referee may only change his decision on realizing that it is incorrect or, at his discretion, on the advice of an assistant referee, provided that he has not already restarted play.

6. Assistant Referees

Parents may be used as assistant referees to help the referee in controlling the game in accordance with the laws of the game.

7. Duration of the Game

U-8 short-sided games are played in halves of 24 minutes each, with quarter breaks within each half to allow for player substitutions. Halftime intervals are as designated by the referee, from a minimum of 5 minutes to a maximum of 10 minutes.

8. Start and Restart of Play

There is no change from regular play, except that opposing players must be 8 yards from the ball when the kickoff is taken.

9. Ball in and out of Play

As in regular play, the *whole* ball must cross the touch line or goal line to be out of play.

10. Method of Scoring

Again, there is no change from conventional play: the *entire* ball must be over the goal line between the goalposts for a goal to be scored.

The score for each game is recorded although not posted. League standings are recorded. All players should still receive participation awards.

11. Offside

The offside law is introduced into AYSO U-10 short-sided soccer and should be adjudicated as in regular play.

12. Fouls and Misconduct

There is no change from regular play, although referees should still work cooperatively with coaches to eliminate the need for yellow card cautions or red card dismissals. No yellow or red cards are shown.

All infractions should be explained to the player or players involved.

13. Free Kicks

There is no change from regular play for either direct or indirect free kicks except that the opposing players must be at least 8 yards from the ball when the kick is taken.

14. Penalty Kicks

Penalty kicks are also introduced at the U-10 level. As in regular play, all players except the kicker and the goalkeeper must remain outside the penalty area (in this case, 8 yards from the ball) until the kick is taken. The goalkeeper's feet must remain stationary on the goal line until the ball is kicked.

15. Throw-In

There is no change from regular play. At this level if a player commits a foul on the throw-in, the throw is awarded to the opposition.

16. Goal Kicks

There is no change from regular play.

17. Corner Kicks

There is no change from regular play except that opponents must be at least 8 yards from the ball when the kick is taken.

U-12 Short-Sided Rules

1. The Field of Play

The playing area should be a maximum of 90 yards long and 45 yards wide. The field is marked in the same way as a field in regular play.

Spectators are not allowed behind either goal or within 3 yards of either touchline. Parents and players can encourage players, but not coach or instruct them, during the course of the game.

2. The Ball

A size 4 ball should be used, 25 to 26 inches in circumference, 12 to 14 ounces in weight.

3. The Number of Players

Each team has a maximum of 9 players on the field at any time, 1 of whom is a goalkeeper. Each team has a maximum of 13 players on the roster. Each player on the roster plays a minimum of 50 percent of the playing time, 75 percent if possible.

Substitutions can be made at halftime or when the referee stops the game midway through each half. Substitutions for injury can be made at any time.

4. Players' Equipment

Appropriate footwear for this age group means sneakers or soft-cleated soccer boots. Shin guards are mandatory for practices as well as games. No player is allowed to take part in practice or a match wearing a cast or splint.

5. Referees

The referee should be either a registered referee or a youth referee and should always emphasize safety, fairness, fun, and learning. AYSO referees are encouraged to explain any infringements to the player or players and assist in familiarizing players with the game.

The decision of the referee is final and must not be questioned by coaches. A referee may change his decision only on realizing that it is incorrect or, at his discretion, on the advice of an assistant referee, provided that he has not already restarted play.

6. Assistant Referees

Assistant referees should be certified assistant referees.

7. Duration of the Game

U-12 short-sided games are played in halves of 45 minutes each, with quarter breaks within each half to allow for player substitutions. Halftime intervals are as designated by the referee from a minimum of 5 minutes to a maximum of 10 minutes.

8. Start and Restart of Play

There is no change from regular play.

9. Ball in and out of Play

As in regular play, the *whole* ball must cross the touch line or goal line to be out of play.

10. Method of Scoring

Again, there is no change from conventional play: the *entire* ball must be over the goal line between the goalposts for a goal to be scored.

11. Offside

The offside law is the same as for regular play.

12. Fouls and Misconduct

There is no change from regular play, although referees should still work cooperatively with coaches to eliminate the need for yellow card cautions or red card dismissals.

13. Free Kicks

There is no change from regular play for either direct or indirect free kicks.

14. Penalty Kicks

As in regular play, all players except the kicker and the goalkeeper must remain outside the penalty area until the kick is taken. The goalkeeper's feet must remain stationary on the goal line until the ball is kicked.

15. Throw-In

There is no change from regular play.

16. Goal Kicks

There is no change from regular play.

17. Corner Kicks

There is no change from regular play.

Chapter 8

For Coaches

The phenomenon of parents and coaches screaming red-faced from the touch lines at each other, at the officials, and at the children struggling on the field casts a dark shadow on youth soccer and children's sports in general and accounts for a startling statistic: 73 percent of kids quit their childhood sports by the age of 13, when the pressures put on them by coaches and parents don't make playing worthwhile any longer.

Moreover, 70 percent of the children who don't return to youth soccer stay away because of unpleasant experiences with the coach. Conversely, 70 percent of those who *do* stay with youth soccer say they continue playing because of positive experiences with their coach. Good coaches leave a lasting impression on players. Unfortunately, so do bad coaches.

Successful Coaching

As soccer becomes a growing obsession for youngsters across the United States, experienced coaches are at a shortage, so more and more soccer moms and dads are finding themselves having to coach a sport they know little or nothing about. This leads many of them on a daunting quest to uncover an answer to the epitome of coaching questions: What does it take to be a great youth soccer coach? Years of experience playing the game? An in-depth knowledge of soccer tactics and formations? Or a degree in child psychology, perhaps? These can't hurt, for sure, but the answer is much simpler than that.

Lawrence remembers Coach Gravett at Danbury Boys. He wasn't a skilled trainer or an astute tactician; he didn't nurture any great players or lead the team to any trophy wins. In fact, he knew less about the game of soccer than most of the players he was coaching. But he did one thing very well. He always kept the game fun for them. Do that as a coach, and you'll leave a lasting and positive impression on your players. Make it fun and the rest will follow.

1. Make the Game Fun

If kids are enjoying themselves, they don't care about the score, the performance, the weather, or anything else. Fun is the primary motivator for children, and they learn more when they're having fun.

In 20 years from now,

The 11 Keys to Successful Soccer Coaching

1. Make the game fun.
2. Promote teamwork, mutual respect, and camaraderie.
3. Praise effort, not results.
4. Keep your expectations reasonable and realistic.
5. Help players learn from their mistakes.
6. Encourage your players to follow the spirit as well as the laws of the game.
7. Always look for positives.
8. Never take yourself or the game too seriously.
9. Be a role model for good sportsmanship.
10. Make safety a priority.
11. Remember, coaches make mistakes too.

none of the kids will remember the score of their youth soc-cer games. What they will remember is the fun they had and the important difference the coach made in their lives.

2. Promote Teamwork, Mutual Respect, and Camaraderie

A sense of belonging to a team helps to develop self-esteem in children. The greater a child's self-esteem, the more confidence he has on the field and the better he is likely to play. Don't allow kids to abuse or ridicule one an-other. You can't make them friends, but you can make them a team. When they pull on that team shirt, they become one and they win or lose as one. All the kids should be recog-nized for their contributions, not just the "star" players. En-courage the striker, for example, to thank the player who provided the assist that enabled him to score.

Do things with your players away from the soccer field—take them to watch an MLS (Major League Soccer) game, or throw a pizza party, for example—that draws them together as a team. One AYSO coach even invited the whole team to his wedding and reception!

3. Praise Effort, Not Results

Every child can put in maximum effort; but not every child can be a great player. If a coach recognizes only the score, then all children will at some point be losers. But if the coach recognizes effort, that leads to an enjoyable, char-acter-building atmosphere. Then all children, regardless of talent, can be winners.

As a coach, Vince would always cheer just as hard when a player made a great tackle as when someone scored a goal.

Acknowledge passes, blocks, and clearances—that will make every player on the team feel appreciated.

4. Keep Your Expectations Reasonable and Realistic

Don't expect too much of players in terms of their time, energy, and performance levels. Younger kids especially have trouble maintaining focus and concentration, particularly during games, when there are so many distractions on and around the field. Teenagers always have plenty of distractions. The players are there to enjoy themselves, not to be buried under the weight of a coach's unrealistic expectations. Commitment and enthusiasm decline in kids of any age when they're not having fun.

> *The best inspiration is not to outdo others,*
> *but to outdo ourselves.*
>
> —Anonymous

5. Help Players Learn from Their Mistakes

Never be sarcastic; never ridicule or yell at a player for any reason. Kids deserve to be treated with the same respect you show other adults. Players need to be allowed to make mistakes. If they're scared of making errors or messing up on a set play, for example, they'll never try new things, attempt new skills. Making mistakes is an integral part of the learning process.

If a player makes a mistake, like scoring an own goal for example, the coach can explain to the player what she did wrong. Say, for example, "Unlucky. You did well to get to reach the ball. Next time, though, try to keep your eye on the ball so you're less likely to slice it." The next time the player is in the same situation, she'll have the confidence to put her coach's words into practice, without being scared of making a mistake.

6. Encourage Your Players to Follow the Spirit As Well As the Laws of the Game

Yes, there are rules, and then there is the spirit of those rules, or why the rules were made. Basically, there are two kinds of rules—the ground rules and the rules of fair play.

Ground rules are just that, rules to give conformity or consistency to the game. For example, every field is marked out in the same way, and penalty area, goal size, ball size, and so on are all the same. The rules of fair play, however, are there to protect players and to ensure equality. Laws on high kicking and dangerous tackles, for instance, protect children. Guidelines for playing children of similar age and talent levels assure the games will be competitive and give every team a chance to do their best.

Unfortunately, rules and regulations can't cover every possible eventuality. The rest is up to the players', coaches', and officials' innate sense of right and wrong, or conscience. The best way to judge what's right or wrong is to ask yourself if you would think an action fair if it were done to your team. If you think yes, then it's probably fair. If no, then chances are it's wrong.

When John was playing a team that was fouling a lot or pulling or tripping off the ball, his coach always told them to keep focused on their own game and let the refs handle the opposing players. "If we fouled one of their players, he still urged us to help that player up," remembers John, "even though the other team never returned the favor."

*For when the One Great Scorer
comes to mark against your name,
He writes—not that you won or lost—
but how you played the Game.*

—Grantland Rice, sports writer

7. Always Look for Positives

Give praise generously and specifically. "Excellent volley, great header" means more to a kid than "Good effort, nice try." When the team plays badly and loses, still try to find the positives from the game—they're always there. Praise the effort, the never-say-die determination, the sportsmanship, the way your players congratulated the opposing team at the end. Being positive takes a decision, a decision to have a positive attitude.

8. Never Take Yourself or the Game Too Seriously

Kids rarely do. Vince has an enduring image of his left back Debbie trying to clear the ball but thrashing it into her own net instead. It was her fourth own goal in three matches. But rather than get upset, she instinctively raised her arms and celebrated as if she had scored in the opponent's goal. Vince roared with laughter. For a couple of hours on a Sunday afternoon, he put himself in his players' shoes and saw life through their eyes. The more he laughed and had fun, the more his players did.

9. Be a Role Model for Good Sportsmanship

Accept defeat as graciously as you accept victory. Treat your players, your opponents, and the officials with respect. It is, after all, only a game.

If you're faced with aggressive parents on the other team, the best way to turn them around is to cheer when their children do well. Demonstrate through your smiles and friendliness that this is not a life-and-death competition, but rather a game for both sides to enjoy. Reinforce your players' good behavior and good sportsmanship: "That was nice of you, Judy, helping the other player up. I am proud of you."

At the end of a game, regardless of whether your team has won or lost, remind parents that:

- Winning is not as important as having fun and developing character.
- It is not important for a child to be the best, but for her to try her best.
- Parents' attitude towards their children's play is very influential, especially for children who are under 10.

It's often hard for one adult to teach something to another adult without sounding righteous. The best thing a coach can do is lead by example. If you suspect a parent will criticize his or her child at the end of a game, make a point of complimenting that child as she comes off the field, before the parent has an opportunity to say anything negative. Often, parents will follow your lead.

10. Make Safety a Priority

Check your equipment and playing facilities. They should meet safety standards and be appropriate for the age and ability of your players. Follow the advice of a physician when determining when an injured child is ready to play again.

11. Remember Coaches Make Mistakes Too

You're not a robot. You'll have off days and make mistakes. Don't make a big deal about it. Just learn from your mistakes.

The image Vince used to have of a coach was of a tall, athletic, all-knowing person who never wavers, never trembles, and never doubts himself. To him, *coach* stood for:

C   Caustic
O   Obviously a leader
A   Always right
C   Come on, make my day
H   He-man

What he discovered after being a coach was very different. "I realized that coaches—great coaches—come in all sizes, genders, and from many different backgrounds." A lot of coaches in soccer have little or no prior knowledge of the sport. *Coach* in youth soccer should stand for:

C   Caring: treats all children equally
O   Objective and organized: capable of building self-esteem
A   Attitude that is always positive
C   Courageous enough to do what is right for the kids
H   Humorous: making soccer fun so that kids want to return

Test Your Coaching Aptitude

Don't be afraid if you are asked to or are considering becoming a coach. Being a coach can bring out the best in you. It can give you the power to make a difference. If you wonder if you have what it takes to be a great children's coach, select *a* or *b* to complete the following:

1. A main objective of youth soccer is:
    a. To win.
    b. To build character and self-confidence in children.
2. Another objective of youth soccer is:
    a. To make great athletes.
    b. To enable children to have fun and make friends.
3. The happiest team is:
    a. The first-place team.
    b. The team demonstrating cooperation and teamwork.

If you answers are mainly *a*'s you're not an AYSO coach. Call the major leagues; they're looking for your type!

If *b*'s are your answers, you are the one we are looking for. You are AYSO material.

How to Be a Youth Soccer Coach

It is character, not talent alone, that will determine a child's "destiny." Youth soccer is just one step in the marathon of a child's life. Youth soccer coaches must subscribe to the philosophy that the role of youth sports is to develop children as complete individuals. They need to be caring people who strive for discipline, who strive to win but, win or lose, will always encourage their players to try their best.

A successful youth soccer coach needs to recognize each

player is an individual with unique needs. To do this, a coach must be *honest:*

H   Honors and respects each child regardless of his talent.

O   Organizes practices and games so that every player on the team has an opportunity to develop and maintain a positive feeling of self-worth.

N   Needs to understand that players want to enjoy attending practices as well as games. If they are not having fun and not learning anything new, kids will lose interest and not return.

E   Encourages, not only when the team is doing well, but especially when the team is losing or the players are discouraged. Being honest with encouragement means a lot to players.

S   Sensitive to players, parents, and referees. Others look to a coach for direction and fairness and an ear that is always available to hear their concerns.

T   Tries to be an example of caring, character, and courage. Stand up for *what* is right, not *who* is right. A good coach is an example. A great coach is an inspiration.

When the coach upholds these principles and helps to develop the children as both players and individuals, the pressure of the game situations become less stressful, less important, and more conducive to the healthy development of kids.

The Meeting: You Make a First Impression Only Once

Anyone who has coached for two or three years realizes the first meeting between coaches and parents is not just *a* meeting but *the* meeting.

Almost everyone remembers the first day at school, the first day on the job, the first customer, and so on. Well, parents seem to remember the first meeting with their kids' soccer coach. The first meeting is usually a time when parents are all ears. For once, at least, they all seem capable of seeing things clearly, objectively. Once the season begins, of course, the honeymoon quickly ends and the pressures and stresses of the game often wash all traces of common sense away. But for that first meeting, the coach has a real opportunity to set the tone for the rest of the season.

Who Should Attend?

The parents, all the parents, not just the moms, but also the dads, should attend. Most importantly, the assistant coaches must attend. Having a parent not understand your philosophy is one thing, but if your assistant coaches don't, you're in serious trouble.

If at all possible, it should be you, the head coach, who makes the calls to the parents and especially to the assistant coaches. Others can do the follow-up calls if necessary.

The Letter

The letter may be the most important contact you make with the parents. It will set the tone of your all-important first meeting. The letter should include the when, where, who, and why:

1. The time and date of the meeting.
2. The location of the meeting—include a map showing directions to your home.
3. Who you would like to see attend, that is, both parents.
4. Then state your philosophy: Soccer is just a game. The object is for the children to have fun, learn new skills, and develop the principles of character.

Here's a sample letter:

Dear Parents,

Welcome to AYSO soccer, one of the first steps in your child's development. It is my intention to make this an enjoyable and memorable experience for both you and your child. To do this I will need your help.

On [time and date] there is a meeting for all parents at [place]. (A map and directions are enclosed.) I cannot stress how important it is that all parents and/or guardians of every child attend. Soccer is more than just an enjoyable sport; it is also an opportunity to bond with your child and teach him [her] important life lessons.

My objectives as your child's coach are to build the 3 C's:

Character. To demonstrate, through my example, the meaning of honesty, responsibility, loyalty, and discipline.

Conscience. To help build your child's sense of right and wrong.

Courage. To encourage your child to follow his [her] conscience, to stand up for what is right, to take responsi-

bility when something goes wrong, and never to be afraid to say, "I made a mistake."

To do this, I need each parent to:

1. Be _present_ as much as possible at practices and games. This is the greatest gift you can give your child.

2. _Understand_ your child is not an adult physically or mentally and grows bit by bit.

3. Have a _positive attitude_. Praise your child's efforts, not the results. Have five positive comments for every negative comment you make.

4. Be _consistent_. Let your words and actions send the same message throughout the season.

5. _Accept_ your child for the gifts given him [her]. Don't make your child responsible for your happiness. Don't worry if your child is not a great player, only if he [she] is not a happy, contented player.

Remember, on my team, winning is not the priority; building the 3 C's—Character, Conscience, and Courage—is. Building ability is secondary to building an honest, responsible, and contented child.

I can't do this without your help. Call me at [phone] if you have any questions.

Sincerely,

Your Coach

P.S. Don't be afraid to remind me of what I said in this letter at any point during the coming season!

Vince and John both agree that their coaching experiences have been some of the most rewarding of their lives. Start off on the right foot and yours will be too.

Conducting the Meeting

Once everyone is assembled, there are two ways to conduct a meeting. Either you can dictate your philosophy and rules, or you can encourage parental participation.

Your philosophy as a coach should acknowledge the role of sports in developing children as complete individuals and instill in the parents the primary purpose of youth soccer—to build character and self-confidence in children, rather than winning games and rewarding talent. Learn and reinforce the five philosophies of AYSO. Explain how parents can help their children obtain these goals, how they can help make the soccer field a field of dreams, and finally how they can handle the most common problems that arise as a soccer parent.

Listen to parents' concerns, learn what their priorities are, and take the opportunity to uncover potential problems that will exist on your team, such as which parents will pose difficulties. For example, there's always at least one parent who insists at the first meeting that his or her child should be the goalkeeper or the striker. Confronting these people early on often prevents future problems. Make it clear that every player will have the opportunity to try every position, to provide the best way of knowing who plays well in what position.

The Test

From an educational standpoint, there's no better way to have people participate, to have them remember information, and to keep them interested than to give them a test. Ask parents the following questions at the first meeting.

"What do you hope your children will learn from their soccer experience?"

The answers are invariably along the lines of the following:

1. To learn to win
2. To learn how to compete and be a winner in life
3. To get talented enough to earn a scholarship to college
4. To make new friends
5. To learn discipline and teamwork
6. To learn how to be a sportsman, someone with character, a sense of right and wrong, and courage
7. To learn that sports are more fun than gangs and drugs
8. To develop confidence and self-esteem

There is nothing wrong with answers 1, 2, and 3, but expect these parents to be potential problems.

Once all the answers are in, don't be afraid to ask every parent his or her opinion, whether that parent's hand is raised or not. Everyone's opinion is important, and everyone's opinion must be heard.

Remind parents that self-esteem and confidence come from building a strong conscience and character. There is always one parent who will try to monopolize a meeting. Feel comfortable cutting that person short, thanking him or her, and reminding parents to try to keep their comments down to less than a minute. Then remind them that you will be available afterwards.

"How can we attain the goal of making your child self-confident?"

The most common responses are "My child will become self-confident . . ."

1. By being on a winning team
2. By being the best
3. By my setting a good example as a parent
4. By having a good coach

The answer you want is this: "Parents can help promote self-confidence in children by creating a harmonious environment, through cooperation with the coaches, and by adopting the four keys to childhood success—be present at the games, communicate clearly with your child, always maintain a positive attitude, and always accept your child for who he or she is."

Ask parents to promise that:

- They will never yell or use profanities at their child or any other child, coach, or referee.
- They will attempt to always give positive encouragement to their child.
- They will watch and listen to their child.
- They will make it a priority to attend practices and games.
- They will remember that coaches do the coaching and parents do the cheering.

"If you have a problem with me or one of our coaches, how would you like us to deal with it?"

Here there is no right answer. Just listen and take the opportunity to find out if any of the children have special needs, like asthma or epilepsy; are on medication; or have any learning difficulties.

Special Situations

Address how parents can deal with some of the most common stressful situations that arise on the soccer field. For example, the opposing team is overly aggressive with very competitive, and sometimes even vicious, parents and coaches. What should you do?

Remind parents that at all times they must treat anger and contempt with respect and calm. Their children are playing for fun and to build character. The parents, therefore, must be good examples and show character themselves, especially when it is most difficult to do so.

Make friends. One way to prevent an overly competitive atmosphere is for parents and coaches of the opposing teams to make friends before the game. Tell your parents to always make sure they go over to the other side prior to the game, shake hands, and ask them about their children.

Cheer when one of the players on the opposing team makes a good play.

When their coach gives strong negative remarks to one of his players, try to find an opportunity to praise that child. Of course, do the same thing for your own team.

Finally, remind parents of the social and emotional reasons why children become involved in sports:

1. To have fun
2. To meet new friends
3. To wear a uniform and be part of a team
4. To learn to improve their skills
5. For the excitement of competition

Practice Sessions

A good coach should plan each practice ahead of time. Try to focus on one particular skill or aspect of the game at each practice. For example, if the team's passing was poor during the last

A Typical Practice ⚽
1. Warm-up
2. Drills (games)
3. Friendly game
4. Cool-down

game, devote an entire practice session to improving the players' passing skills. A typical practice can be divided into four parts: (1) warm-up, (2) drills to learn or improve one particular skill, (3) friendly game to practice the new skill, and (4) cool-down.

1. Warm-Up

Soccer is one of the safer sports, regarded as a "medium injury sport," where participants are less likely to sustain injury than in baseball, basketball, or football. According to the American College of Sports Medicine, however, nearly half of all injuries sustained in youth sports are preventable. Warming up before and cooling down after games and practice sessions not only help prevent injury but also help with body conditioning and organization and teamwork. Just remember: always do some light exercise before stretching the muscles.

Warm-Up for U-10 and Younger

Younger children are far less likely to get hurt playing soccer than older kids. Getting the attention of children in the U-6, U-8, and U-10 age groups and organizing them for practice is much more of a concern for coaches. One answer is to have enjoyable warm-up routines that prepare the kids physically and focus their attention on the coach. The emphasis is more on fun and less on flexibility. It's very rare for kids this age to pull muscles, so stretching is generally unnecessary.

Try warming them up with a variation of a "Simon Says" game. For example, when you precede an instruction with the words "Coach says"—as in "Coach says, do five jumping jacks"—they have to follow your command. However, if you just say, "Reach for the sky," they don't have to do that. Not only does this get the kids warmed up, but it also gets them organized and gets their attention firmly focused on you.

Warming-up exercises can also be great for team spirit if they are performed with a song or some type of chant.

Remember, for the younger groups it is not important that they do the exercise in unison. Kids this age are usually all jumping up and down at different times like spilled marbles bouncing on the pavement, and many don't know their left from their right. Don't be upset; just be happy they are performing the exercises and having fun doing them.

Warm-Up for U-12 and Older

It is important that older players are taught good habits and get used to warming up and stretching before games and practices. A warm-up should last 10 to 20 minutes, gradually increasing in intensity.

Suggested Stretches

A slow, progressive stretch held for 20 to 30 seconds is best. Bouncing can do the opposite of stretching and lead to injury. Bouncing causes a stretch reflex to go to the spinal cord and tells the muscle to shorten and contract. Bouncing will, therefore, make it harder to stretch or elongate a muscle and can cause a muscle tear or even a tendon or ligament to tear that might not be noticed until the child begins to run. **Caution:** Do not bounce!

Calves. Take one step forward, bend the front knee and, keeping the back straight, push the heel of the back leg into the ground. Repeat with the other leg.

Hamstrings. Take one step forward and bend the back knee. Place both hands on the back leg and lean forward so the stretch is felt at the back of the straight leg. Repeat with other leg.

Quadriceps. Stand on one leg, keeping the knees close together. Hold the ankle and bring the heel of the bent leg towards the butt, feeling the stretch in the front of the thigh. Repeat with other leg.

Groin. Take a long step forward and, keeping the back straight, move the weight down and forward so the stretch is felt in the groin area. Repeat with other leg.

Waist and back. Lie on your back, arms spread wide. Bend both knees and move them slowly to one side, feeling the stretch in the lower back and abdomen. Repeat, moving to the other side.

Shoulders. Link both hands and reach above the head. Keep the back straight and move the arms slightly backwards until the stretch is felt in the shoulders.

Neck. Tilt the head slowly to one side, keeping the neck straight. Hold to feel the stretch in the opposite side of the neck. Repeat to the other side.

<u>Running</u>

Since soccer involves sprints and stop-start exertion, coaches should concentrate more on short shuttle runs and sprints than on long jogs. In a typical soccer game, players will sprint for 50 yards, jog for a while, and then suddenly sprint again. Conditioning should be geared to this kind of exertion. Circuit and interval training is more suited to soccer than long, steadily paced runs.

2. Drills (games)

Drills need to be competitive—kids enjoy competing, regardless of who wins—but not boring or repetitive. If it's a drill to practice ball control, such as having small groups of players passing the ball to each other without letting the ball touch the ground, build in a competitive element. Each time a player lets the ball hit the ground, he has to do five push-ups, or the winner is the person who lets the ball hit the ground the fewest times.

Vary the drills so that players all get to do something they're good at. Vince was never very good at juggling the ball and so didn't enjoy it when they did "who can juggle the ball longest" drills. But Vince was an accurate passer and so enjoyed the drills that focused on that skill.

3. Friendly Game

Gear the game to focus on the skill that was practiced during the drills. If the drills concentrated on passing the ball, for example, then focus on passing during the game by, say, introducing a one-touch or two-touch rule. One-touch means that players can touch the ball once, but then can't touch it again until another player has done so. This forces them to make first-time passes without controlling the ball. Two-touch allows them one touch to control the ball and another to pass.

4. Cool-Down

At the end of a game a cool-down is important. Without it, cramps and sore muscles, or even injury to joints or muscles, can occur.

After a game, muscles that have been stressed and have built up lactic acid and other toxins must be nurtured in order to remove these toxins and stresses. Suddenly stopping may cause a muscle to contract, preventing blood supply that is needed to remove and extract toxins. This can cause cramping and, later on, sore, painful muscles and even future injuries to joints and connective tissue.

Once again, the cool-down is most important in the older age groups. It is done by two methods.

1. Gradual decrease in exercise.
2. Literal cooling-down with icepacks.

The gradual cool-down is done by a gradual walk for 1 to 2 minutes after the game. Advise your players to stand, not sit or lie down. Gradual stretches, similar to the warm-up stretching, but limited to 5 seconds, can also help.

Cold packs can be applied to injured areas such as bruised shins, hips, or thighs. Use the cold pack, not directly placed on the skin, but over a towel, for 15 to 20 minutes. This is especially useful on joints and can help prevent long-term injuries, especially if there has been a sprain.

Injuries

The role of youth coaches is one of injury prevention and not treatment of injuries. All but minor injuries (bumps and bruises) must be evaluated by competent medical personnel before an injured player is allowed to play after surviving an injury. In youth soccer, the most frequent injuries are:

1. Heel pain due to repetitive activity on the heel (twisting and turning during the course of a soccer game), especially during a growth spurt. Fracture is less likely, but should be looked into if pain is a persistent problem.
2. Osgood-Schlatter's disease of the knees. This is a painful bony swelling just below the knee.
3. Shin splints, which is pain along the front shin bone that increases with exercise.
4. Tendonitis, especially of the Achilles tendon at the heel. Other places are the knee and groin areas.
5. Sprain of the ankle or knee.
6. Bruising due to a kick or tackle.

The more a child plays one particular sport, the more overuse syndrome is likely to occur. The most frequent are those noted above.

Since children's bones are not fully grown, ligaments and tendons pulled repeatedly at the ankles, heels, and knee can cause pain and persistent injury.

Treatment should include rest, sometimes prolonged rest for a month, also icing and anti-inflammatory medication. If a symptom persists more than three days, a doctor should be consulted. If it persists for more than a week, orthopedic or neurological evaluation may be required.

R-I-C-E: Rest, Ice, Compression, and Elevation

In general, a child who is limping and is no better after 5 minutes of *rest* and a trial walk and trot should not play. *Ice* should be immediately placed on the area. *Compression* with an elastic bandage can reduce swelling and subsequent injury to the area. *Elevation* of the limb will help. Elevation with the heel above the knee or groin is sufficient, or elevation can be above head level.

Finally, physical therapy is very important to prevent re-injury.

> **R-I-C-E**
> ⚽
> For sprains, strains, or contusions remember *R-I-C-E:*
>
> R Rest
> I Ice
> C Compression
> E Elevation

Head Injuries

If a player sustains a knock on the head, the coach should *immediately* examine him. The player should take no further part in a game if either of the following happens:

1. He is knocked unconscious for any period of time.
2. He is dazed and momentarily doesn't respond correctly to these questions—
   a. What is your name?
   b. Where are you?
   c. What is the year, month, or day?
   (Remember the questions have to be appropriate to the age of the player you are dealing with).

Signs of a Concussion
⚽

These may include any or all of the following.

1. Loss of consciousness
2. Inability to concentrate or maintain eye contact
3. Disorientation—the child is unaware of the time, place, or people around him
4. Repeating the same question, such as "Where am I?"
5. Unsteady walking
6. Headache
7. Vomiting
8. Unequal pupils

Always look for good eye contact and the ability to concentrate. A player who cannot maintain eye contact with you or seems to stare is showing indications of concussion. **Caution:** The child should not be playing any further and should be taken to a hospital for *immediate* medical attention.

Caution: If any of these symptoms occur, take the child immediately to a hospital to be evaluated by a doctor. A child with loss of consciousness and sudden vomiting and unequal pupils is an extreme medical emergency.

Chapter 9

For Parents

A girls' soccer league in Ohio recently enforced a noise ban on all parents watching from the sidelines during one day's play. Parents could only respond to goals, fouls, and other incidents with a smile, a nod of approval, or a shake of the head. The day of silence was the league's attempt to put youth soccer back in perspective. The report noted that the kids had a great time that day and were "able to make decisions on their own without being questioned or yelled at."

This may be an extreme solution, but if you're a parent who's new to soccer or you're a little unsure what is expected of you during a game, remember how much the kids in Ohio enjoyed that day of silence. Soccer is an emotional game, littered with tragic examples of how some people have let that emotion run riot.

On May 24, 1964, a riot broke out in Lima, Peru, during an Olympic qualifying game with Argentina. By the day's end, 318 men, women, and children were dead, and more than 500 were injured. On June 27, 1969, El Salvador defeated Honduras to qualify for the World Cup, sparking a full-scale military conflict between the two nations. The death toll exceeded 2,000. On July 2, 1994, Colombian defender Andres Escobar was shot to death on a Medellín street for scoring an own goal during his team's World Cup defeat by the United States.

As bizarre as these events are, they do illustrate how some people take soccer way too seriously. Perhaps sadder still is what happened in New Jersey on September 11, 2000, when a tied soccer game between 8- and 9-year-old boys ended in a brawl among their parents. An argument over a penalty shootout escalated into a fistfight, with as many as a dozen parents and coaches becoming involved before police were called to the scene. Unfortunately, this is not an isolated incident. More and more often, youth sports events are marred by the behavior of parents. Yes, soccer can be a very emotionally involving game for a spectator, especially for a parent watching his or her child. But it's still a game, just a game.

How to Be a Great Soccer Parent

Kids want their parents to watch them play soccer. They don't want them to gossip to the other parents, or spend the whole game talking on a cell phone or reading a book. And they certainly don't want them to yell instructions or argue with the referee or the opposing coaches. Just watch the game. It can be as enjoyable and rewarding to watch a game of youth soccer as it is to play.

1. Remember: Your Child Just Wants to Have Fun

Remember that your child is the one playing soccer, not you. It's very important to let children establish their own goals—to play the game for themselves. Take care not to impose your own standards and goals on them.

Don't put too heavy a burden on your child to win games. Surveys reveal that 72 percent of children would rather play for a losing team than ride the bench for a winning team. Lawrence played on a winning high school team that was about as much fun as boot camp, as well as the very mediocre Danbury Boys team. It's easy to tell which one he enjoyed the most. Children play for the fun of playing.

2. Don't Be a Sideline Coach or Referee

Kids hate parents shouting instructions at them, even if the parents know what they're talking about. Often your kid is too busy concentrating on the game to hear you anyway, and if you shout even louder, you just end up embarrassing him or her. The only voice a player want to hear is the coach's.

Arguing with the coach or the referee may seem like an act of support to some parents, but to kids it is nothing more than a waste of time and a cause of acute humiliation.

If a player hears her parents question the coach's decisions or disparage the coach's efforts, she'll lose respect for that coach. If she hears her parents shout abuse at the ref, she's likely to do the same. Of course,

> ### The 11 Keys to Being a Soccer Parent
>
>
> 1. Remember: Your child just wants to have fun.
> 2. Don't be a sideline coach or referee.
> 3. Always be positive.
> 4. Support your child.
> 5. Accept your child.
> 6. Never compare your child to others.
> 7. Keep your expectations realistic.
> 8. Be on time for practice and games.
> 9. Make safety a priority.
> 10. Emphasize effort over winning.
> 11. Promote sportsmanship.

referees make mistakes; that's an integral part of all sports at all levels. You want your child to learn to be a good sport, so don't blame losses on the referee.

Where appropriate, ask the coach to clarify exactly what is expected of you and what you are entitled to expect from the coach. Remember, refs and coaches are just volunteers; they are there solely for a love of soccer and kids. Be considerate of the people taking time out to work with your child. Let the coaches coach and the refs ref.

3. Always Be Positive

Parents serve as role models for their children. Become aware of this, and work to be a positive role model. Applaud good plays by your child's team *as well as* good plays by the opposing team. Avoid becoming frustrated or focusing on players' failings.

John's worst experience in youth soccer occurred during a U-14 game. He was at the far post defending an in-swinging corner. He tried to clear the ball out of danger, but he momentarily took his eye off the ball and ended up slicing it into his own net. His coach and teammates consoled rather than rebuked him, but then he heard two voices screaming at him from the touch line. "I looked up to see Paul's parents, red with anger, yelling all manner of insults at me for scoring an own goal. I was mortified. Even after play resumed, I could still hear them shouting abuse at me." This continued through the rest of the second half. Every time he was on the ball on their side of the field, they shouted at him. As a 13-year-old, he had no comeback. He just snarled at them and tried to avoid the ball for the rest of the game, terrified at what their reaction might be if he made another mistake.

As an adult, John finds it just as difficult to understand

their behavior. What kind of people do that to a kid just for making a mistake on the soccer field? Negative comments have no place on the field or the sidelines. "I speak from painful experience," says John. "I still cringe at the mere recollection of that game."

4. Support Your Child

Supporting your child by giving encouragement and showing interest in the team is very important. Even if they have had fun and played well, kids still prefer to win rather than lose. Maybe allow them some quiet time after a game to think about things; then help them see the positive aspects of the game, like the effort they put in, the fun they had being with their teammates. Positive reinforcement is the best way to help children achieve their goals and overcome their natural fear of failure. Nobody likes to make mistakes. But it's all part of learning, so encourage a child's efforts and point out the good things he or she accomplished.

Help your child work toward skill improvement and good sportsmanship in every game. Kids love learning something new, especially when a parent teaches it. Encourage your child to accept responsibility for his or her own performance and behavior. Don't blame losses on a teammate or a bad refereeing decision or a coach's mistake. Your child is part of the team and so shares equally in the losses as he does in the victories.

5. Accept Your Child

Parental approval and acceptance are hugely important to children. Your child might not be the most talented soccer player and he may not play for a winning team, but he or she can still be a success in your eyes, if success is judged by effort and perseverance. Everyone has good qualities as well as not-so-good ones. Accepting a child without condition, good qualities and bad, empowers the child and builds self-esteem and self-confidence regardless of the level of talent.

6. Never Compare Your Child with Others

Parents often compare their child with other players on the soccer field—those who appear to be the most talented—and judge their own child negatively. If Christine can control the ball like that, why can't my child? Children develop at different rates, and of course some develop certain skills better than others. Christine might be a talented soccer player, but your child is probably better than her at something else.

Not every child can be a great soccer player. But every child can enjoy the game and learn the value of effort and determination.

7. Keep Your Expectations Realistic

Parents consciously or unconsciously believe that their child must be everything they were, be as great as they were (or think they were). Maybe they have dreams of parenting a World Cup winner or professional athlete. These unrealistic expectations can burden a child, crippling him with a fear of being rejected by the parents for failing.

Parents who have expectations that are not congruent with the child's ability can take even the most highly motivated child and drain him or her of all confidence and self-assurance. Keep your expectations reasonable. Expect your child to have fun, to play with commitment, and to develop self-confidence on and off the soccer field. These are the important things. Anything beyond that is just gravy.

8. Be on Time for Practice and Games

Being on time is a courtesy to coaches—so they don't have to keep repeating instructions every time a late arrival turns up. It's also courteous to the other players, so they don't have to interrupt practice drills or start the game without the whole team assembled.

9. Make Safety a Priority

Make sure cleats are clean, in good condition, and appropriate for the playing surface—molded studs for normal playing conditions, plastic or aluminum screw-in studs for very wet or slippery fields. Have shin guards and other equipment packed and ready to go for practice or games.

Be sure your child eats a balanced meal the night before a morning game or the morning before an afternoon game. Bring plenty of water or sports drinks to the field, especially on hot days. And remember that in cold weather kids lose body heat faster than adults, so have a sweatshirt ready after practice and games.

10. Emphasize Effort over Winning

Praise effort and performance more than results. Emphasize the importance of striving to win rather than winning itself. Teach your child that hard work and an honest effort are often more important than victory—that way, your child will always be a winner despite the outcome of the game!

If you're not present at a game, the first question you should ask the child when he or she comes home is "Did you have fun?" or "Did you play well?" not "Did you win?"

11. Promote Sportsmanship

Parents are the most important role models kids have. Always promote the positive aspects of the sport, such as fair play, and never condone violations of the laws of the game or behavior that breaches the spirit of the laws. Children learn sportsmanship through the example of parents and coaches. They learn by watching and listening, so always keep a positive outlook and demonstrate good sportsmanship by supporting the coaches, referees, and players on both teams, despite any mistakes they may make during the course of a match.

Parents need to demonstrate:

- The fun of hard-fought but fair competition
- How to win graciously
- How to lose graciously
- How skills and abilities can be improved through practice and hard work
- The social skills involved in being a member of a team
- The importance of acknowledging good play by teammates and opponents
- Gratitude towards the coaches and referees that donate their time and energy to the good of kids and soccer

Why Soccer? Why Sports at All?

It's important for parents to assess why they have their child in soccer and to understand what participation in soccer can potentially mean for their child, both now and in the future.

Stop and ask yourself why you want your child in a soccer league. Here as some frequently cited reasons:

1. Everyone else's children are in soccer.
2. It is a great babysitting service while I get my shopping done.
3. Maybe my child can get a scholarship and, who knows, become a wealthy pro soccer player.
4. I can show off my superior genetic lineage.
5. It's a great way for my child to meet new friends.
6. It's time that I can share with my child to bond.
7. It's a chance for the family to support one another.
8. It's an opportunity to help my child deal with the realities of life, which include both victory and defeat.

Well, if you picked 1 through 3 and admit it, you're at least truthful. There is hope for you. If you answered yes to number 4, there are other sports you might prefer having your child participate in—like bare-knuckle boxing.

If you picked 1, 2, and 3, but after reading 5 through 8, think those are what you really want, then youth soccer is the place for your child.

Youth soccer is an opportunity for children to have fun, make friends, improve their fitness and academic abilities, increase their self-confidence, learn teamwork and social skills, and develop character.

Fitness

Almost 50 percent of preadolescents are overweight. For many kids, eating excess food can be a habit, as much as smoking is a habit, and like smoking, it can lead to illnesses such as heart disease and cancer.

Fitness has two parts:

1. It keeps weight down by burning calories.
2. It increases the capacity of the cardiovascular system and, just as importantly increases neurotransmitters (nerve juices) in the brain to make one feel healthy, energetic, and happy.

Exercise is a major treatment for depression as well as for weight gain. It lowers bad cholesterol and increases good cholesterol. It reduces blood pressure, increases heart capacity, and decreases heart disease. It can also arrest osteoporosis, cancer, and possibly Alzheimer's disease, the major cause of memory loss in the aged.

Soccer offers plenty of running and provides the opportunity for a child to establish good exercise habits for life. It pulls your child from the three most common fatteners:

1. Sitting in front of a TV
2. Playing computer games
3. Snacking while doing either of the above

Youth soccer brings your child onto the field of fitness where his mind, as well as his body, is exercised.

Yes, Mom and Dad, your children might not know it, but just by taking them out to the soccer field you have pointed them in the direction of a longer, healthier, and therefore possibly happier life.

Academic Achievement

Youth sports in general are directly related to academic achievement. Statistics show that children who play active sports are:

- 57 percent more likely to finish high school
- 40 percent more likely to go to college
- 37 percent less likely to become involved in delinquent behavior at school
- 88 percent less likely to be negatively involved with the police

In organized sports like soccer, children are provided with the tools to excel in any endeavor. They are taught discipline and responsibility and are rewarded for effort. Soccer teaches citizenship and loyalty and teamwork—all the tools to develop a better society and a successful child.

Character

A recent nationwide survey of 8,600 U.S. high school students conducted by the Josephson Institute revealed the following statistics:

- 71 percent of all high school students admitted they cheated on an exam at least once in the previous 12 months.

- 92 percent lied to their parents in the previ-ous 12 months; more than one in four (27 percent) said they would lie to get a job.
- 40 percent of males and 30 percent of fe-males say they stole something from a store in the previous 12 months.
- Nearly one in six (16 percent) said they had been drunk in school during the previous year.
- 68 percent said they hit someone because they were angry in the past year, and nearly half (47 percent) said they could get a gun if they wanted to (60 percent of males).

Youth soccer organizations like AYSO have recognized the need to teach and promote the principles of character as Vince Fortanasce outlines them in his invaluable book, *Life Lessons from Soccer*. The game of soccer has been described as "an unscripted drama" or "an improvised play," and we would certainly agree with that. Like any play or movie, a game of soccer is a reflection of our lives, and while players are on the field, there is a wealth of opportunity to learn and demonstrate the principles of good character.

What Is Character?

Character, in the long run, is the decisive factor in the life of an individual and of nations alike.
—Theodore Roosevelt

Character is the ethics, values, and habits that a person dis-plays; the way he responds to challenges, obstacles, success, and failure. The Josephson Institute of Ethics has categorized the qualities of good character into the Six Pillars of Character.

1. Trustworthiness

This covers the principles of honesty, integrity, promise keeping, and loyalty. For example, when the ball comes off a player's leg before going out of bounds for a throw-in or corner, the

> **The Six Pillars of Character**
>
> 1. Trustworthiness
> 2. Respect
> 3. Responsibility
> 4. Caring
> 5. Fairness
> 6. Citizenship

player concedes possession without trying to convince the ref that the ball came off his opponent last.

If a child promises to be at practice, parents need to make sure he learns the importance of keeping that promise.

2. Respect

Respect includes dignity, courtesy, tolerance, and acceptance. A player doesn't, for example, argue with his coach or the referee but respects and accepts their decisions. Parents can help teach respect by demonstrating it themselves—refraining from arguing or abusing coaches, officials, or other parents—and by encouraging politeness in their child, insisting on the use of "please" and "thank you."

3. Responsibility

Accountability, obligation, dependability, and the pursuit of excellence are part of responsibility. Players demonstrate responsibility by striving to win, giving every game their best effort, but accepting defeat as graciously as victory. Don't set a poor example by blaming defeat on the referee or a bad coaching decision.

Kids get annoyed when their parents preach good sportsmanship but then blame defeat on an unfair refereeing decision. Be consistent. Players need to learn to accept responsibility for the mistakes they make on the field and off it.

4. Caring

Caring encompasses the qualities of compassion, consideration, giving, sharing, and kindness. Encourage your child to help up an injured opponent, for example. But let her see you do the same. Cheer for the other team when they make a good play; commiserate them if they lose or make a mistake.

5. Fairness

Fairness is demonstrated by impartiality, consistency, and equality. Players need to treat their teammates equally, regardless of their abilities or position on the team. Each player is equally important. Don't let your child feign injury on the field, or cheat in any other way.

6. Citizenship

Law-abiding behavior, community service, and protection of the environment are citizenship responsibilities. In the context of soccer, this means following the laws of the game and the spirit behind those laws. In a wider context it means kids need to see their parents partake in, not just talk about, performing charitable services.

Both parents and coaches teach the Six Pillars of Character. Everything an adult does sends a message to kids. Throwing temper tantrums, screaming at the ref, or bending the rules is an implicit ratification that these actions are admirable qualities, indeed, qualities to be emulated.

Hints for Teaching Character

1. Be an example. Children see what you do, not what you say. Character is taught by example, not just by words. Be responsible, be on time, and be respectful to the referee and the players, parents, and coaches on both teams.
2. Recognize and try to rise above your own competitive and self-serving instincts. Remember, your child plays youth soccer to have fun and learn, not to live out your thwarted ambitions.
3. Every dilemma or conflict on the soccer field is an opportunity to teach and demonstrate character. Tell your kids: If the ref mistakenly awards a free kick to you when you know there wasn't a foul, own up. If a player consistently fouls you, don't retaliate; just concentrate on your own game.
4. After a game, raise issues that occurred during the game. Praise your child if he handled an issue well, or discuss how he could have handled it better, or the lessons he can learn from the incident.
5. Admit when you're wrong. Everyone has shortcomings and makes mistakes. Let your child see that you're not afraid of admitting yours. It will in-

crease her trust and help develop a healthy self-image.

6. Reward your child for his effort and for demonstrating good character, rather than for winning.

The Roles of the Soccer Parent

Having a child involved in youth soccer is a commitment. Not just a commitment to sport, but a commitment to your child and your child's team. This commitment will include being a taxi service, personal assistant, fan, and friend.

Taxi Service

If you have more than one child, be prepared to travel. Get a calendar and try to allow yourself an extra 15 to 30 minutes so you can avoid the mad dash to the field that leaves both you and your child in disarray. Carpooling when you have more than one child, at times, is the only alternative.

Personal Assistant

The major reason why many young children drop out of soccer is a bad experience with the coach. A close second is lack of parental preparation. A child will have a difficult time enjoying him or herself if just prior to the game you go through the great scavenger hunt. "Where are your shin guards? Your socks? Your shoes?" Remember the five *S*'s from bottom to top: *s*hoes, *s*ocks, *s*hin guards, *s*horts, and *s*hirt.

The other equipment needed may be a water bottle and soccer ball. The night before, get a bag and make certain everything is packed away. On a weekday practice or game, this routine can be a lifesaver.

Remember, children younger than 10 are distractible. Despite your telling them a thousand times, they may not have anything ready. This is normal. They're not being undisciplined, unappreciative, or lazy. At this young age, their brain development is such that they are easily distracted and naturally forgetful.

So, it falls to the parents to ensure that everything is packed and ready. If parents are consistent enough, kids will develop a good habit by 10 years of age. If parents always leave it up to their kids, there will be confusion.

Children who are berated or yelled at for being lazy or disorganized immediately before a game will rarely enjoy themselves.

Start on the right foot by being prepared.

Fan

You are your child's number one most important fan. When a parent is present, a child plays better, is more enthusiastic, and smiles more. Most parents bring out the best in their children; others, unfortunately, burden their children.

What is the single most important thing children remember about youth sports? Their parents' presence, or lack of it, which is a major factor in the development of the child's self-esteem. After all, how important can a child feel if mom and dad never go to a game while all their friends' parents are always there?

Friend

A coach, a neighbor, or a buddy can help as a shoulder to cry on, but there's no shoulder as comforting as mom's or dad's.

If your child is a goalkeeper who made a mistake, or an outfield player who missed an easy chance or an important tackle, you may well have to deal with the agony of disappointment and defeat. This child will need consoling.

Remind your child that it's just a game. All that is important is that he tried. Share with him a similar experience that you've had. This is a true opportunity to bond with your child and one he will always remember. Then do something that's fun: go to a movie or out for pizza.

For the goalkeeper, perhaps the most apt to feel blame, remind her the ball must get by all the other players on the team before it passes her. So any goals scored are the responsibility of the whole team, not just her.

AYSO tries its best to ensure every player is in the action for three-quarters of the game, so no child is made to feel left out. Remember, a child's sense of self-worth, especially when the child is under 12 years old, depends much more on your *reaction* to him than whether he is second string or not.

Tell your child that being a utility player, one who backs ups others at any position, is very important. Let him know that you love him and never compare, or allow any one else to compare, your child with other children.

If you do feel affected by your child's being second string, then help him work on his skills. Just make sure it's fun and you don't burden them with unrealistic expectations. Discourage your child from just quitting. Unless there is a very good reason, quitting is a bad habit to develop.

AYSO Safe Haven

AYSO has developed a child and volunteer protection plan called Safe Haven, a program designed to address the growing need for child and volunteer protection.

The goal of the Safe Haven program is to provide a nurturing environment for children and give parents the security that every reasonable effort is being made to ensure that AYSO soccer will be safe, fun, and fair.

Child Protection

There are four elements in the Safe Haven intervention cycle. These are intended to stop child abuse and its agents before they get into the program.

1. Create policies.
2. Screen volunteers.
3. Train volunteers.
4. Promote education and awareness.

AYSO Certification

AYSO's goal is to provide certification training for all its volunteers. Certification offers the hope that every AYSO child will be treated with understanding, compassion, and respect.

Chapter 10

For Referees

Referees, like parents and coaches, are role models. Everything a coach, parent, or referee does and says communicates a message to the players—and that message should always be the same: Fun and sportsmanship are always more important than the result. Referees and assistant referees are responsible for ensuring that players are provided with a fair, fun, safe, and positive environment in which to play.

How to Be a Great Youth Soccer Referee

1. Always Remember That the Game Is for the Players

Player safety and fair play come first. Emphasize enjoyment and good sportsmanship before, during, and after the game in all your interactions with players. Support players' endeavor with positive encouragement. Commiserate with a player if she makes a mistake; congratulate a player if she

---

The 11 Keys to Being a
Youth Soccer Referee

1. Always remember that the game is for the players.
2. Study and learn the laws of the game.
3. Encourage and enforce the AYSO philosophies.
4. Respect other referees' decisions.
5. Have the proper uniform and equipment.
6. Maintain good physical condition.
7. Stay calm.
8. Know a referee's duties.
9. Support good sportsmanship.
10. Always be fair and impartial.
11. Remember Law 18.

---

makes a good play. But make sure your comments are spread equally between the two teams.

Referees need to ensure that players have the correct equipment as outlined in Law 4, and make sure a player does not wear anything dangerous to either himself or others.

Good referees develop positive feelings of self-worth in the children and in themselves.

Inspect the field of play before a game and be aware of potential hazards such as:

- Goalposts crossbars, and nets (the most common source of injury in soccer)
- Walls, fences, and the like near the field
- Sprinkler heads
- Seating in the coaching or spectator areas
- Foreign objects on the field—broken glass, debris, and so on

Whenever a young player appears to be injured—whether you think it's serious or not—stop play to check it out. If the injury warrants, or if there is an open wound, ask that the player be taken off the field. Players who are bleeding must leave the field.

2. Study and Learn the Laws of the Game

Help fellow referees do the same. Know and properly apply the laws of the game.

- Understand and follow all age-specific rules and regulations.
- Stay updated on rule and law changes and interpretations, and equipment improvements. The FIFA Web site (www.FIFA.com) carries the latest revisions of the laws; AYSO also issues information in mailings.
- Attend regular refereeing training courses and regional meetings scheduled through AYSO.

3. Encourage and Enforce the AYSO Philosophies

Especially enforce the philosophies of "Everyone Plays," "Positive Coaching," and "Good Sportsmanship." Recognize and compliment sporting behavior on the part of players, coaches, and spectators. Stress that foul or abusive language will not be tolerated under any circumstances.

AYSO referees are responsible for completing game cards that denote how long each child has played during a game. If, at the end of the third quarter, for example, a coach has overlooked a child and not played him for at least 50 percent of the game, politely point out this oversight so that the child gets to play in the last period.

4. Respect Other Referees' Decisions

Never publicly criticize another official. Respect your assistant referees, whether they are trained assistants or untrained volunteers. The referee is always the decision maker during a game and can and should overrule an assistant referee if he has good cause. However, continually reversing the decisions of an assistant referee undermines the assistant's authority over the players, sets a bad example, and may well cause him to be reluctant to signal infringements when he sees them. Trust and respect the decisions of the assistant referees. Make them part of your team as much as possible.

5. Have the Proper Uniform and Equipment

Wear the proper uniform, and keep it in good condition. Like a police officer or nurse, you'll find it harder to achieve the respect you deserve if no one can distinguish you.

The referee's equipment should include:

- Shirt, shorts, socks
- Coin
- Whistle
- Watch
- Pencils
- Yellow and red cards
- Flags

- Copy of the rules of the game
- Copy of AYSO or age-specific rules
- First-aid kit   } Coaches should provide
- Water and ice } these for the players

6. Maintain Good Physical Condition

Be in good physical condition so you can keep up with the action and properly control a match. Establish a physical training regimen that will maintain at least a minimum level of fitness.

Referees should also warm up properly before officiating a game, get sufficient rest, and drink plenty of fluids.

7. Stay Calm

Maintain control when confronted with emotional reactions from players, coaches, and parents. Demonstrate respect for players, coaches, spectators, and fellow officials.

Exhibit self-control and self-discipline at all times, and recognize the effect your behavior has on players, coaches, and spectators. A referee's role is a difficult one, at times unappreciated by those who like to blame all their own failings on the person with the whistle. Stay in control by screening comments from the sidelines and remaining focused on the game. Keep a sense of humor as well. If a coach is screaming abuse at you from the touch line, appreciate what an idiot he's making of himself and don't be afraid to politely but firmly ask him to stop.

8. Know a Referee's Duties

The referee is charged with many responsibilities. These are some of them.

- Honor accepted game assignments; most Assignors want to be notified so they can assign the replacement (at the proper level).
- Enforce the laws.
- Keep score and time.
- Control substitutions.
- Stop play for injury.
- Suspend or terminate the match for due cause.

Provide a match report if disciplinary action is taken or any other incidents occurred before, during, or after the match.

9. Support Good Sportsmanship

Ensure that players, coaches, and parents show positive respect for the rules and your authority. Acknowledge acts of sportsmanship with a kind word to players, coaches, and parents of both teams. If players are continually criticizing each other, stop play and urge them to work together as a team rather than against each other. If a coach is being negative or abusive towards his players, stop the play and ask him to stop that behavior.

10. Always Be Fair and Impartial

Avoid conflicts of interest. If the coach of one team is your neighbor or the other coach backed into you in the parking lot, don't let your predisposition towards the team cloud your judgment. Decisions based on personal bias are dishonest and unacceptable.

Good referees always provide honest decisions and positive encouragement while ensuring that the rules are enforced in a fair and unbiased manner.

11. Remember Law 18

When you read the laws of the game, you see that there are 17 laws. But every referee must be aware of the unwritten Law 18: The Law of Common Sense.

The purpose of the laws is to provide a framework to promote the game's spirit—that it is fun, fair, and safe. This means the laws are there to facilitate play, not inhibit it. As a referee, ask yourself the following:

- Is it safe?
- Is it fair?
- Does it promote fun?

Make your decisions by answering yes to all three and using common sense.

Why Become a Referee?

Without a judge, there is no court. Without the referee, there is no soccer. The central reasons for becoming a referee are no different from the reasons for becoming a player or a coach. Become a youth soccer referee:

1. To have fun
2. To help teach kids the laws and the spirit of the game

3. To develop children's character, sportsmanship, and sense of self-esteem
4. For a love of kids and the game of soccer

Unfortunately, good referees are rarely remembered. They referee so fairly and efficiently that players, coaches, and spectators hardly notice they're there. They keep the game flowing; they don't make many mistakes (at least no glaringly obvious ones); and everyone's attention remains on the players and the game rather than the official referee. It's the bad referee that always grabs the headlines and sticks in the memory.

Not surprisingly, then, one of the few referees Vince can clearly remember was a terrible one, a young guy of about 18 or 19 who refereed a Danbury Girls game against United in the U-12 season. He had memorably straight, greased-back hair, so we'll call him Curly.

Curly blew his whistle every 5 or 10 seconds, penalizing Vince's team for every tackle, every slight physical contact. Noticeably, however, the United players were allowed to run roughshod over Vince's players, kicking their ankles, pulling their shirts. Every time Vince complained, the ref would stop the game and arrogantly lecture him about the rules of the game. Lecture Vince! A man who had coached for years!

The game descended into a farce. Vince's players were unable to play without being penalized and had more free kicks awarded against them in the first half of that game than they did in all the other games in the season combined. At the end of the half, they were battered and bruised, and one or two of the girls were even reduced to tears by Curly's domineering attitude and blatantly unfair officiating. Vince took the halftime break as an opportunity to have a quiet discussion with Curly. He complained that his players weren't getting any protection from the referee and that the United players were getting away with all kinds of fouls and misconduct. "Someone is going to get seriously hurt," Vince pointed out.

Curly turned to him and began another patronizing lecture on the rules of the soccer. "Besides," he added as an afterthought, "my dad's team never plays dirty."

Referees are certainly in a position to ruin a game. Don't become a referee if your motivation is anything like Curly's:

1. To exert power
2. To physically, mentally, or emotionally dominate others
3. To give your favorite team an edge

Officiating the Youth Soccer Game

For a referee, a game of youth soccer includes the following responsibilities.

Pregame Conference with Assistant Referees

Whether you are working with trained assistant referees or untrained volunteers from the sidelines, take a few minutes to tell them exactly what is expected from them and how they can help you during the course of the game.

Inspecting the Field

Inspect—or have the assistant referees inspect—the field before play to ensure it complies with all safety standards.

Remove any debris. No one should play on the field until it is safe to do so.

Inspecting the Players

Check that all the players' equipment complies with Law 4. Check for rings, watches, bracelets, and so on. At the same time, have one assistant check players' footwear and the other check their shin guards.

Pregame Talk to Players

> ### The Referee's Responsibilities
> ⚽
>
> - Pregame conference with assistant referees
> - Inspecting the field
> - Inspecting the players
> - Pregame talk to players
> - Coin toss
> - Keeping time
> - Positioning
> - Adjudicating fouls and misconduct
> - Supervising substitutions
> - Ending the match
> - Postgame ceremonies
> - Record keeping
> - Postgame conference

Keep any pregame speech short and to the point. The players are there to play, not listen to you recite *Hamlet*. Emphasize fun, fair play, safety, and individual responsibility, and say everything in under a minute.

Coin Toss

Have the captain of each team join you in the center circle. The captain of the visiting team calls the toss while the coin is in the air. The winner chooses ends; the loser's team kicks off.

Keeping Time

Start keeping time from the moment the ball is touched at the opening kickoff, stopping only for substitutions and at halftime. Do not stop keeping time when the ball goes out of play, or you will end up interrupting the action to enforce the laws. If players are deliberately time-wasting, add time on at the end of each half.

Positioning

A simple way for referees and assistant referees to position themselves during play is to follow the diagonal system of control as illustrated in the diagram.

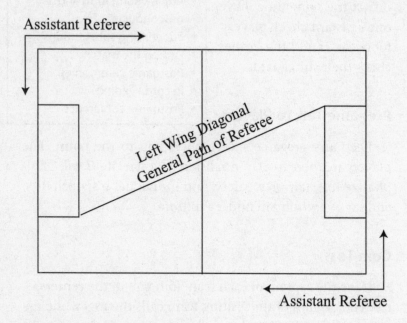

Adjudicating Fouls and Misconduct

Penal fouls, as outlined in Law 12, are penalized by a direct free kick (Law 13) or penalty (Law 14). Nonpenal fouls, also outlined in Law 12, are penalized by an indirect free kick (Law 13).

Positioning at Set Plays

Set Play	Referee Position	Lead Assistant	Trail Assistant
Kickoff	Just outside center circle in the half of the team kicking off.	In line with second-to-last defender or at halfway line.	In line with second-to-last defender.
Goal kick	Midfield or near where you think the ball will land.	In line with second-to-last defender.	At goal kick end: first at 6-yard line; when ball has been correctly placed, move to 18-yard line.
Corner kick	In corner of penalty area or behind goal line between 6- and 18-yard line.	Outside corner flag or on goal line, as instructed by referee.	In line with second-to-last defender or at halfway line.
Penalty kick	On field in line with 6-yard-line between goal area and edge of penalty area to (1) ensure kick is taken properly, (2) watch for encroachment, and,	At intersection of goal line and penalty area facing the goal to see if ball crosses the line for a goal.	At halfway line ready to move quickly into position in line with second-to-last defender.

(continued)

Penalty kick *(continued)*	(3) ensure goalie does not advance illegally.		
Free kick, near goal	On or near diagonal, near the wall to watch for infractions and judge offside.	At goal line or in line with second-to-last defender.	In line with second-to-last defender or at halfway line.
Free kick, not-near goal	Roughly on diagonal to judge en-croachment and reach center of play quickly.	In line with second-to-last defender.	In line with second-to-last defender.
Throw-in	On referee side of the field: move slightly off diagonal toward the touch line. On assistant referee side: move from diagonal toward center of field.	In line with second-to-last defender.	In line with second-to-last defender.

Handling the ball is a penal foul, but one often misinter-preted by referees. If a player deliberately strikes, holds, moves, catches, or deflects the ball with hands or arms, that's a penal foul. If the ball strikes the player's hands or arms, which is more often the case, the player has committed no foul. It's especially important to remember that young players have a tendency to cover their faces or other parts of their body with their hands for protection when the ball is coming at them with some force. Referees should bear this in mind when ruling on a hand ball violation.

Show yellow and red cards in accordance with the laws of the game.

The AYSO national referee program recommends that children should not be cautioned or sent off except under extreme condition. Referees should consider whether children in this age group are fully aware of their actions, and that they can usually be controlled by a verbal admonishment before a caution or sending off becomes necessary.

Supervising Substitutions

When a substitute replaces a player, that substitute becomes a player as soon as the substitution procedure has been completed.

A proper substitution procedure is made by following these steps:

1. The referee, assistant referee, or fourth official is notified of the intended substitution by the coach.
2. At a stoppage in play, the referee calls for the substitution.
3. The player leaves the field.
4. The referee signals for the substitute to enter the field of play.
5. The substitute enters the field at the halfway line.
6. Upon entering the field, the substitute becomes a player.

AYSO regulations modify both the number of players and the substitution procedure as part of the "Everyone Plays" philosophy. Substitutions are allowed only at these four times during play:

1. Midway through the first half.
2. At halftime.
3. Midway through the second half.
4. For injury at any time.

To allow for substitutions midway through each half, the referee should wait until the ball goes out of play rather than stopping play at the exact midpoint of each half.

Ending the Match

When the allotted time and any additional time added at the end of the game for substitutions or time wasting has expired, the referee whistles to indicate the end of the game.

Postgame Ceremonies

Some regions organize postgame ceremonies, such as handshakes or high fives. Referees should remain vigilant for any acts of poor sportsmanship, such as a player spitting on his palm before high-fiving an opponent.

Record Keeping

Referees should take a few moments after the game to complete game cards, lineup cards, or roster cards while the game is still fresh in their mind.

Postgame Conference

Confer briefly with the assistant referees to congratulate and thank them. Clarify any decisions they were unclear about. Take the opportunity to teach and build teams.

Tips for Referees

- Do not stay on a strict diagonal. Move off as necessary to stay close to play without interfering.
- Try to keep play between you and your assistant referees.
- Try to keep an eye on players off the ball.
- Learn to anticipate situations. For instance, look to the assistant referee if the potential for offside exists.
- Maintain eye contact with your assistant referees as much as possible.
- Indicate in some way when you intend not to honor an assistant referee's signal.
- Modify your positioning to suit the age and skill level of players involved.

Tips for Assistant Referees

- Assist, don't insist. Do not expect the referee to always agree with you. If you are overruled, support the referee's decision.
- During the normal flow of the game, position yourself in line with the second-to-last

defender or the ball. Always follow the ball to the goal line. It's your responsibility to signal a goal.

- If the referee allows a goal and you disagree, stand perfectly still at attention, flag at your side, until the referee responds or restarts the game.
- If the ball enters the goal, but the referee allows the game to continue, raise the flag above your head and hold until the referee responds.
- Keep your attention on the game. Don't get into discussions with coaches or spectators.

Tips for Referees and Assistant Referees

- Enter and leave the field together as a team.
- At halftime and fulltime, retrieve the ball and meet in the center circle to complete the record keeping.
- Respect and support each other, the players, the coaches, and the spectators at all times.

Referee Signals

Caution or sending off:
The referee holds a
yellow or red card
above her head.

Play on/advantage:
The referee waves play on
with her hands to show
that she is applying the
advantage rule and play
should continue.

Direct free kick: The referee points in the direction the kick is to be taken.

Indirect free kick: The referee raises her hand.

Assistant Referee Signals

Substitution: The assistant referee signals to the referee that a team would like to make a substitution by holding her flag overhead.

Throw-in:
The assistant referee points the flag in the direction the throw-in is to be taken.

Offside on the
near side of
the field.

Offside in the
middle of
the field.

Offside on the far side of the field.

Chapter 11

For Players

How to Enjoy Youth Soccer As a Player

1. Play for the Fun of It

Play because you enjoy the game not just to please your parents or coach. If you would rather be playing a different sport, let them know. Chances are they won't be angry; they just want you to enjoy what you do.

If you do decide to play, remember soccer just a game. You're there to have fun, make friends, and to learn sportsmanship.

If I do one awesome thing a day, I try to feel good about that. It's better than feeling bad about the eight things I didn't do too well.
—Brandi Chastain

2. Play by the Laws of the Game

Learn the 17 laws of soccer. The more you know about the rules of the game and the more you adhere to those rules, the more you'll enjoy the sport. Never condone violations of the rules from your teammates.

3. Never Show Dissension

Never argue with or complain about referees' calls or decisions. Soccer is often played at a fast pace. Things happen quickly, so of course the ref is going to make mistakes. And sometimes those mistakes seem glaringly obvious to the players on the field, and sometimes they might even cost you the game. But that is as much a part of soccer as a bad bounce or a lucky deflection. It's something you can't control. Once the referee has made a decision, he'll never change his mind because a player argues with him or abuses him. So keep your concentration, and don't waste your time and energy arguing with the ref.

Lawrence can only recall being cautioned and sent off once. But that was enough. There's no honor or pride in being ejected from a game. It was the closing minutes of a game at home to Broomfield Lions, a team much higher in the league than Danbury Boys. The Lions were leading 2-1 and playing well. Then their striker burst past the Danbury right back and dribbled the ball into the penalty area. Paul, the other Danbury center back, and Lawrence

---

The 11 Keys to Enjoying Youth Soccer As a Player

1. Play for the fun of it.
2. Play by the laws of the game.
3. Never show dissension.
4. Don't retaliate.
5. Be a team player.
6. Show good sportsmanship.
7. Try your best.
8. Respect your opponents.
9. Cooperate with your coach.
10. Practice as hard as you play.
11. Always adhere to the spirit of the rules.

quickly closed in on him from different directions and clumsily tackled him at the same time, making him the meat in their "sandwich" before sending him sprawling to the turf. The referee immediately blew for a penalty and proceeded to show Paul and Lawrence the yellow card for dangerous play.

Paul was an extremely aggressive kid and reacted badly to the caution. He cussed and cursed at the referee. It was more uncharacteristic for Lawrence to show dissent to a ref, but in the heat of the moment and perhaps spurred on by Paul, he, too, rudely shouted his disgust at the ref. "Ultimately, I was angrier at myself for giving away a penalty at the end of a game we were winning than at the referee for his decision," remembers Lawrence. "Nevertheless, Paul and I left the ref with no choice but to caution us both a second time and show us the red card." With only a couple of minutes remaining in the game, they were sent off.

As he trudged off the field, Lawrence glanced over at Coach Gravett. "He didn't say anything, but I could sense the disappointment in his expression. I knew I'd let him down."

The Lions scored from the penalty to tie the game up at 2–2. Then in the remaining minute they launched another attack. With only 9 players left on the team, Danbury was outnumbered, and with 2 defenders suddenly missing, they were completely disorganized at the back. With the last kick of the game, the Lions scored again to win the game 3–2. Lawrence felt dreadful. His ill-disciplined outburst had not only resulted in his dismissal, but had cost his team a well-deserved victory.

His teammates didn't rebuke him for throwing the game. Most offered consolations, suggesting the ref overreacted. But Lawrence knew the ref hadn't overreacted. He had. It was a bad tackle and a worse response. "The least I could do after letting the team down was accept responsibility for my actions."

4. Don't Retaliate

Control your temper and resist the temptation to retaliate when you feel you've been wronged. This happens most games. A player fouls you, and the ref doesn't see it. That's part of the game. If a player consistently fouls you and the ref doesn't penalize that player, it's easy to lose your temper and retaliate. But remember, anger can have a negative effect on a player's performance. If you're concentrating on getting back at another player or swinging out with your arm, you're not focusing on the ball or the game. And if you do retaliate, chances are the ref will spot it and you'll be cautioned or sent off. Either way, you're rewarding your opponent's dirty play. The only way to beat it is to control your temper and get on with the game.

When John was on the receiving end of bad tackles and niggling fouls from an opponent, he would resist the urge to retaliate and maintain his concentration on the game by silently chanting "my ball, my ball" to himself. That way, he refocused his attention on gaining possession of the ball rather than retaliating against the offending opponent.

5. Be a Team Player

Concentrate on playing soccer with your best effort. Work equally hard for your team as for yourself. If you're a striker and your defense is under pressure, drop back to help out. Remember that the goals of the game are to have fun, improve your skills, and feel good. Don't be a showoff or a ball hog.

Understand the other players' roles within the team. If you understand how difficult the striker's job is, you're less likely to get annoyed when he or she misses an easy chance. If you appreciate the demands on a goalkeeper, you're more likely to sympathize when he or she lets a soft shot in.

Encourage your teammates; never criticize them for making mistakes. Everyone on the team is equally important. You win together and lose together.

 We do a lot of team-building exercises. If you look at our gold medal game, it came down to who wanted it more. At the end of the day we just wanted it more, because we'd been through so much together.
—Shannon MacMillan,
on the U.S. Women's 1999 World Cup win

6. Show Good Sportsmanship

Be a good sport by cheering all good plays, whether by your team or your opponent. Treat all players as you would like to be treated. Congratulate the opposing players at the end of the game if they won, or commiserate with them if they lost. Play to win, but not to win at all costs.

A fabulous example of sportsmanship occurred in a recent professional game. In the last minute of a tied match, Italian striker Paolo Di Canio had the opportunity to shoot into an open goal. As the ball was played into him in the opponent's penalty area, he saw the goalkeeper collapse with a serious injury. Rather than take the opportunity to score the winning goal, he instead caught the ball and signaled for the trainers to give medical attention to the goalie. The entire crowd was stunned, and supporters from both teams gave Di Canio a standing ovation at the end of the game. He received more congratulations and applause from an act of sportsmanship than he ever had from scoring a goal. It's worth remembering.

7. Try Your Best

That's all anyone can ever do or expect from you. And you'll be surprised how far that will get you, in life as well as in soccer. Put every ounce of effort into a game, try your very best, and great things will follow.

Crowds at professional soccer, while they always appreciate the skillful, flamboyant players, often seem to applaud loudest for the player who gives 100 percent effort all game, every game; the player who keeps trying right up until the final whistle. This may not be the player who can dribble past five opponents and then score with a spectacular long-range shot, but is more likely the one who keeps tackling, keeps urging his or her teammates forward, the one who somehow manages to scramble in a last-second equalizer through sheer willpower. Players like that always seem to inspire their teammates around them. And the great thing is every player can play like that, regardless of his or her skill level.

It's striving to win that matters, not winning itself.

Nothing in the world can take the place of persistence. Talent will not: Nothing is more common than unsuccessful men with talent. Genius will not: Unrewarded genius is almost a proverb. Education will not: The world is full of educated derelicts. Persistence and determination alone are omnipotent.

—Anonymous

8. Respect Your Opponents

If an opponent beats you, don't make excuses; just accept it graciously. If you win, don't gloat or put down your opponent. It doesn't matter how good a player you are, or how good your team is; there will always be someone who is better.

John prided himself on his pace when he played as either a midfielder or defender. He knew that an opposing player would rarely if ever beat him in a foot race to the ball. If an attacker ran at him with the ball, he was always confident he would be able to make the tackle. "If he wanted to score, he was going to have to go past a different defender—I wasn't letting anyone by," says John. "Then I faced the Dolman twins."

They were strong, fast, and incredibly skillful. One brother played in midfield and destroyed our midfield single-handedly. The larger brother was a center forward whom John was responsible for marking. In the opening 5 minutes, they both chased onto a through ball played toward John's goal. "He beat me to the ball, which surprised me enough. Then, when I dived in for the tackle, he shrugged me off with incredible ease. All I could do was stare forlornly, chin down in the mud, as he ran through the rest of the defense and banged home the first goal."

By halftime John was shell-shocked. "We were down 4–0, and the Dolman center forward, despite my trying to tackle him, had scored every goal. I couldn't believe how good this guy was." In the second half, things improved. Dolman finally missed a few shots, and John managed to get the odd tackle in on him. But both brothers never stopped reminding everyone of the score or who the better players were. They were as arrogant as they were talented.

Years later, John heard that both the Dolman twins had been signed by a professional club. As incredible a player as the center forward brother was, he played just once for the first team, coming on as a substitute. His twin didn't even get a game. The club released them at the end of the season for simply not being good enough. John believes their "arrogance and lack of respect for opponents might have had something to do with it as well."

9. Cooperate with Your Coach

Listen to your coach and follow your coach's directions. One person has to have the final say in how the team plays, who plays where and when. That person is your coach. You might not always agree with the coach's ideas and opinions, but you're a team and you have to operate as one unit under the guidance of the coach. If you have disagreements with the coach, discuss them with him or her quietly and calmly in private after practice or a game. Never publicly argue or lose your temper with the coach. It will only serve to disrupt your team.

10. Practice As Hard As You Play

The goals of soccer are to have fun and improve your skills. Turn up to practice on time—let your coach and teammates know you're committed to the team. Put in 100 percent effort, and you'll be surprised how quickly your skills and your understanding of the game improve. There's no pressure at practice, so you can try new things and make plenty of mistakes.

Lots of [players] are afraid that if they make a hard tackle,
they are going to make the [teammate] mad. Or they're
afraid if they score a goal, their teammates will
get mad. . . . But we go out and try to make
the other player work hard, and to do that
you have to give it your best. When we go against
each other, we are, like, "I'm going
to give you my best shot to help you out."
—Tisha Venturini, U.S. Women's Team,
on practicing hard

11. Always Adhere to the Spirit of the Rules

Respecting the spirit of the rules is all part of being a good sport. Victory is always a hollow one if it's earned as a result of unfair play. Play to the rules and to the spirit of the rules. One of the worst sights in professional soccer is to see a player feign an injury to get an opposing player cautioned or dismissed, or to see a player dive to the ground after little or no contact in the hope of winning a free kick or penalty. To see kids emulate that behavior in youth soccer is particularly disturbing.

Playing soccer in any position can get rough, but particularly so in midfield, where most games are won or lost. Tackles fly in; fouls are made. That's all part of the game. Never practice or condone behavior contrary to the spirit of the game. There's no need to emulate cynical professional players who dive exaggeratedly as soon as an opponent comes near them or roll around feigning serious injury after they've been tackled. The only thing to do is pick yourself up and get on with the game.

How to Handle
Disappointment and Defeat

So, they told you that soccer was fun, that you would get to hang out with your buddies and enjoy competing against other teams. What they didn't tell you, though, was that soccer sometimes isn't fun, like when you've just made a bad pass that's led to the opposition scoring the winning goal and knocking your team out of the playoffs. A whole season, all the hopes and dreams that you and your teammates had of lifting the cup suddenly vanish with one mistake, and all your parents can say is "Cheer up. There's always next year. It's not the end of the world."

They're wrong, of course. There isn't always next year, and to a 12-year-old it is pretty much the end of the world—at least briefly. So what do you do?

Vince coached the Danbury Girls in the Cup Final at the U-12 level. The game was against their archrivals, the Dynamo, and was played at a professional stadium. "It was the biggest Sunday of my players' lives," he remembers. "And it turned out to be the most disappointing. They lost 2–0."

At the end of the game, the Dynamo players jumped around in celebration and Vince's players trudged off, heads dropped, tears trickling down a few faces. Vince ran out to the players and told them to hold their heads up. They had played well, given it their best shot, he said, and he was proud of them. He directed them to shake hands with the Dynamo players before retreating to the locker room.

It was a tough defeat to swallow. Cup finals, even for above-average teams, come around about as often as the Messiah on the back of a comet. Nevertheless, Vince didn't want his players' solemn expressions to ruin the experience for the Dynamo players. They had played well and deserved to win—any crying or complaining from his players was to be kept at bay until they were back in the locker room.

"There's always next year," Vince told them. And he was right. Not about next year—they never made it to the final again—but about the attitude they should adopt. When the final whistle blows, you no longer have any control over the result. All the missed chances, the silly mistakes, the decisions that went against you count for nothing. "All you can control is the way you react," says Vince.

Remember, good sportsmanship is always more important than winning.

After a tough defeat, take a few minutes on your own to vent your anger and disappointment. Then calm down and remind yourself of the following:

1. There are some things you can't control, like winning and losing. If you could, then everyone would win every game and winning would mean nothing.
2. The things you can control are the amount of effort you put into a game and the amount of fun you get out of it. If you didn't play with as much effort as you can, vow to try harder in the next game.
3. You're not alone. All your teammates feel just as bad as you do. Why not concentrate on cheering them up instead of focusing on your own feelings? Congratulate them all on their effort; vow to all try harder next time.
4. Soccer is only one part of your life. There are so many other things you enjoy doing as well. If you

made a mistake and people are blaming you, remember that they're only criticizing a tiny piece of what makes up "you."

5. Don't compare yourself with others. So one of your teammates or someone on the other team is a better passer or scores more goals or saves more shots than you do. So what? You're probably better at something else than they are. All you can ever do is try your best.

The Only Thing That Matters

Since they played together as a team of 9- to 16-year-olds, the Danbury Boys grew up and moved thousands of miles apart. Lawrence has seen two of his teammates—Babs and Den—get married; he found out Paul, the aggressive midfielder, became a traffic cop when Paul pulled him over on the freeway not so long ago (no, Paul didn't give him a ticket); Lawrence is godfather to center back Pat's daughter, and he drives a car that's still registered to the left back, Dave.

Look around at your teammates. Can you imagine them grown up, with responsible jobs and marriages and children? Imagine in 20 or 30 years' time, still being friends with them when you're the same age as your parents are now, sitting down together and saying, "Aw, do you remember that playoff game, the one we lost . . . ? "

And you'll laugh and joke about the mistakes you all made, or the refereeing decisions that went against you, or the tactics the coach came up with. You'll all remember it differently. Some of you will remember exactly who scored and how; others won't even remember the result. One thing's for sure, though, none of you will care about how many trophies you won or didn't win, who gave away a bad penalty, or who missed an easy chance. The result of every youth soccer game you've ever played in won't mean a thing to any of you by then. Because you'll remember just one thing, the only thing that counts: How much fun you all had playing soccer together.

Chapter 12

A Brief History of Soccer

Origins of the Game

Various forms of soccer-style games have been in existence around the world for thousands of years. The ancient civilizations of China, Japan, Greece, Rome, Egypt, and Northern Europe have all laid claim to the origins of soccer, or "football" as the world outside the United States calls the game. However, the world's most popular sport, in its modern form, is generally believed to have originated in England.

The earliest accounts of the game in England date back to the Roman occupation, when rival church parishioners used the skulls of their conquerors as a ball. In later years the ball became the head of a sacrificial animal and was kicked about by competing villages. By the 1300s, however, the game had lost all sense of decorum and was played by huge, unruly mobs barraging through town and village streets, and goals were scored by literally *any* means possible. Such was the mayhem, bloodshed, and property damage caused by these mob games that King Edward II threatened to imprison anyone caught playing "the Fute-ball" as it was known. The rulers of Scotland and France soon laid down similar decrees against soccer, but royal disapproval did little to quell the burgeoning popularity of the game in Europe.

Soccer in its modern form, however, didn't begin to take shape until the early 1800s, when it was introduced into English public schools and colleges. In 1823, at Rugby School, legend has it that William Webb Ellis, supposedly out of frustration, picked the soccer ball up and ran with it, thus creating the "handling game," or Rugby football (the forebear of American gridiron). The creation of the English Football Association in 1863 clarified the rules of this "kicking" version of the game, and it became known as "Association Football." With it came also the creation of the term "soccer." The common schoolboy slang of the day added -*er* or -*ers* to the root of words. For example, breakfast was known as "brekkers," rugby was referred to as "rugger," and association football became "soccer" from the "soc" in "association."

With the game established in England, it quickly spread across the globe via the vast British Empire. The simplicity of the game and the lack of equipment needed made it a catchy export, and soccer mushroomed in popularity, with the British ex-patriots forming clubs and associations all around the world. In 1882 the football associations of England, Scotland, Wales, and Ireland formed the International Board to standardize the rules of the game. The national associations of Holland, Denmark, New Zealand, Argentina, Chile, Switzerland, Belgium, Italy, Uruguay, and Germany quickly joined them. The United States followed in 1913.

In 1904, with games between nations already commonplace, the world governing body of soccer, the Fédération Internationale de Football Association (FIFA), was formed.

The World Cup

FIFA held the first international tournament in 1930, signaling the dawn of the World Cup era and the advent of soccer's holy grail. Thirteen nations competed in the first World Cup finals, with an average attendance of 24,139 for the 18 games. The popularity of the tournament has increased every time, and in 1998, 32 teams earned a place in the month-long tournament in France, watched by an average TV audience of 578 million viewers per game. A staggering two billion people, or one in three human beings on the planet, watched the 1998 World Cup Final itself!

The History of Soccer in the United States

The earliest account of a soccer-style game in the United States dates back to the arrival of the Pilgrims, who observed up to a thousand native New England Indians playing with a ball on a wide stretch of beach. The Indians called the game *pasuckuakohowog,* meaning "they gather to play ball with the foot." But it was the British who introduced the modern version of soccer to the United States.

Curiously enough, the United States was the first former British colony to start playing soccer in the nineteenth century, primarily at upper-class schools and colleges. The Oneida soccer club, formed in Boston in 1862, was the first soccer club to be established outside England, even predating the formation of Scottish teams. As in the early days in England, rules varied widely among different schools and communities. Princeton University, for example, played with as many as 25 players, and other colleges played the game with innings, like baseball, and awarded victory to the first team to score a fixed number of goals.

The first intercollegiate game using rules resembling modern soccer was played between Princeton and Rutgers on November 7, 1869. Interestingly, this same game is also generally recognized as the first American football game as well. The second such intercollegiate game was played with an oval ball under English rugby football rules, and marks the evolution of soccer into the modern American gridiron game. In 1894, the first fully professional soccer league was established by a group of professional baseball owners who wanted to fill their baseball stadiums during the off season. Unfortunately, the league collapsed under heavy financial losses during its inaugural season.

A second league, the National Association Football League (NAFBL), was formed in 1895 but lasted only four seasons. It was revived in 1906, two years after a U.S. team won the gold medal at the 1904 Olympic Games, but it wasn't until the 1920s, considered the first golden era in U.S. soccer, that a viable league, the American Soccer League (ASL), was formed.

In 1930, the United States participated in the first World Cup in Uruguay. After the demise of the first American Soccer League, the game continued primarily on a semiprofessional and amateur level, with many of the most successful teams being tied to ethnic communities. From these ethnic communities, a highlight of U.S. national men's soccer arose.

In 1950, the United States qualified a second time for the World Cup finals. The U.S. soccer federation assembled a ragtag team of immigrants' sons to take part in the tournament in Brazil. Only one had ever played professional soccer; the others included a meatpacker, a school teacher, a dishwasher, a knitting machinest, a paper stripper, and two mailmen. On June 29, 11 of these no-hopers lined up in a packed Brazilian stadium to face England, rated as the finest soccer team in the world and hailed by the Brazilian papers as the *reyes de futbol* ("kings of soccer"). Against all the odds, the U.S. amateurs pulled off what is still considered to be the greatest upset in World Cup soccer history by beating England 1–0.

Despite such glory overseas, U.S. soccer continued anonymously at home through regional semi-pro leagues and the low-key American Soccer League II. Under the threat of bankruptcy in 1968, the ASL merged with the United Soccer Association, becoming the North American Soccer League (NASL). Respectable crowds were attracted to many games, but the league overspent on expensive international stars, like Pelé and Johan Cruyff. The foreign imports were highly skilled and brought a great deal of recognition to the game, but simply cost too much to be supported by the existing fan base. Player costs gradually bankrupted one team after another until the NASL folded in 1984.

Ironically, with the sport floundering at the club and national levels, grassroots participation in soccer mushroomed, particularly with youngsters. National organizations such as the AYSO soon eclipsed all but the most established sports in youth participation levels.

Soccer Spreads Across the United States

The renaissance of soccer in the United States came in 1990, when the men's U.S. National Team took its place among the 24 qualifiers for the World Cup finals for the first time since that historic tournament in 1950. The United States was also awarded the 1994 World Cup on the condition that a national professional league would be established.

With the U.S. National Team assured of qualification as host nation, the players prepared for the tournament by winning the inaugural U.S. Cup in June 1992, defeating Ireland, 3–1; defeating Portugal, 1–10; and tying three-time World Cup champion Italy, 1–1. The following year's U.S. Cup was then used as a dress rehearsal for World Cup organizers, officials, and volunteers, as well as the U.S. National Team. Once again the team made headlines around the world when it again defeated England, this time by an even better score of 2–0. Attendance and media interest were high, with 286,761 people attending the tournament's six games, and ABC-TV broadcasting the June 13 U.S.-Germany match live. Plans for Major League Soccer were unveiled by U.S. Soccer Federation president Alan Rothenberg to follow the U.S.A. hosting of the 1994 World Cup. On June 4, more than 91,000 fans jammed the Rose Bowl in Pasadena, California, to watch the United States defeat Mexico, 1-0, in its final warm-up prior to the World Cup.

The 1994 World Cup proved to be the biggest event ever in U.S. soccer. More than 3.5 million fans flocked to stadiums across the country for the tournament—breaking the attendance record established in Italy in 1990 by more than one million—and soccer fever in the United States was at an all-time high. The U.S. team advanced beyond the first round for the first time in 64 years, falling to the eventual champion, Brazil, 1–0, in a close game; having tied Switzerland, 1–1; defeated Colombia, 2–1; and narrowly lost to Romania, 1–0, in the opening round.

In 1996, Major League Soccer (MLS) successfully kicked

off, and the U.S.A. finally had a national professional league. Major League Soccer established a unique corporate structure whereby teams are managed by investors and exist as separate franchises, but the league manages all player signings and salaries. The MLS also retains control of allocating players and approving trades to ensure parity in team lineups. To promote the development of U.S.-born players, the MLS also imposed a limit of five foreigners per team.

If 1996 and the launch of MLS were triumphs for U.S. soccer, 1998 and failure in the World Cup proved a disappointment. Dissension between national team players and Coach Steve Sampson resulted in substandard performances on the field, and the United States was swept out of the 1998 World Cup finals in France in the opening round.

Back on the domestic front, the MLS has blossomed with renewed sponsorship deals and TV contracts, and by the year 2000 the primary league in the United States had, for the first time ever, gone five straight years without losing or moving a franchise. Coupled with widespread participation at youth level and the success and popularity of the women's game, soccer looks set for a bright future in the United States.

The History of Women's Soccer

When I was playing, they said soccer was a man's world and that women should remain on the sidelines. All I can say is I'm glad I never had to go up against Mia Hamm.

—Pelé

Like the men's game, women's soccer started in the late 1800s, when it gained popularity with teams in Canada, England, and France. During the 1920s, U.S. colleges played club or intramural women's soccer. However, women's soccer has, until very recently, struggled with negative or nonexistent media coverage. In 1921, the English Football Association even banned women from playing on its soccer grounds. Even at the 1996 Olympic Games in Atlanta, the only women's soccer game even partially televised was the final match between the United States and China, despite the fact that a crowd of more than 80,000 attended the game.

Soccer became a popular sport for young girls in the United States during the 1950s. Then, in the 1960s, Eastern European Communist countries began encouraging women's soccer as part of the Communist drive to dominate all sports by both sexes. England finally lifted its ban on women's teams in 1969, and by 1971, there were 34 countries playing organized women's soccer. The first unofficial women's world cup was held in Mexico that same year.

In 1972 the U.S. Congress passed Title IX of the Educational Amendments Act, watershed legislation for women's sports in general, soccer in particular. The law decreed that no school could receive federal funds if it discriminated against women in any educational activities, including athletics, and became the driving force behind an explosive growth in women's college soccer and the resulting success of the U.S. Women's National Team.

By 1991, 65 countries sponsored women's teams, and the first official FIFA Women's World Cup was held in China. The U.S. Women's National Team qualified for the world championship by defeating its five CONCACAF (Confederation of North, Central American, and Caribbean Association Football) opponents by a combined score of 49–0. The team went on to capture the World Cup with a 2–1 win over Norway on November 30. It was the first world title ever won by U.S. women's team. The Women's World Cup was an unbridled success, with exciting, competitive games, sell-out crowds, and a worldwide television audience. In England, the organization that had once banned women's soccer, now actively supported the game.

The second Women's World Cup was held in Sweden in 1995, and despite a disappointing loss to Norway in the final, the women's game in the United States was really starting to come into its own. In 1996, women's soccer had a significant breakthrough, when it was included in the Atlanta Olympic Games, again drawing huge crowds to witness another triumph for the U.S. team.

Just five years after hosting the men's World Cup Final, the United States provided the stage for the 1999 women's tournament. It was an unprecedented success, the greatest women's sporting event ever, garnering unequaled world attention and averaging 38,000 fans per game, which even surpassed attendance for the 1982 men's World Cup. The U.S. women again secured the championship with a nail-biting victory over China on penalty kicks. The final, held at the Rose Bowl, attracted the largest crowd ever for a women's sporting event and secured a sizable TV audience. More Americans watched their women lift the 1999 Women's World Cup than watched the 1999 NBA (National Basketball Association) finals.

When, a few minutes after 5 P.M. pacific time on July 10, 1999, AYSO alumna Brandi Chastain netted the winning penalty kick and became an instant sports icon by tearing off her shirt, a nation came to realize that football doesn't just mean the NFL (National Football League). The Women's World Cup, the U.S. team, and the game of soccer had finally captured the attention of the U.S. public and media.

The Growth of AYSO

Since its establishment in 1964, AYSO has continued to grow and offer its membership relevant programs.

In 1971, two San Fernando Valley, California, residents developed AYSO's first girls' program. Today, a corporate sponsor has joined with AYSO as the organization's first official sponsor of its national girls' initiative. Currently, 40 percent of AYSO's players are girls. That's up 10 percent in ten years and nearly double the percentage since the mid-1980s. U.S. National Team stars Brandi Chastain, Julie Foudy, and Joy Fawcett all came up through AYSO programs.

In the mid-70s, an AYSO coach chartered new territory as he welcomed the organization's first player with Down's syndrome. As a result of this landmark union, soccer was introduced into the Special Olympics. Today, AYSO offers its membership the Very Important Player (VIP) program for kids with special needs. VIP boasts 75 programs and 1,500 players.

In 1995, two AYSO parents established the first AYSO program in Moscow. Today, the Moscow program has almost 500 registered players. In addition, an AYSO program was started in Puerto Rico in the spring of 1998 and another in American Samoa in 1999.

AYSO is supported by more than 250,000 volunteers. Parents donate their time as coaches, referees, administrators, or sponsors. In 1998, AYSO unveiled its new Coach Certification and Safe Haven Programs. Each was designed to strengthen the organization's role in child protection. Although AYSO is primarily a youth sports organization, it realizes the importance of providing a safe and healthy atmosphere for children. AYSO is continually working to improve the education of its volunteers in the fields of child development, human behavior, and sports psychology. A strong emphasis is placed on ethics and sportsmanship and the development of the whole child.

AYSO is an association member of the U.S. Soccer Federation (USSF), the national governing body for soccer in the United States. Through the years AYSO has also maintained relations with organizations such as the National Council of Youth Sports, Girl Scouts USA, the National Association for Sports and Physical Education, People to People, Optimists International, Police Athletic Leagues, the National Alliance for Youth Sports, Boys and Girls Clubs of America, the YMCA, and the Character Counts program. In addition, AYSO works closely with 20 corporations that are part of the organization's National Team of Sponsors.

AYSO is the leader in establishing groundbreaking youth soccer programs in the United States. The organization is proud to have paved the road for youth soccer and looks forward to meeting the challenges of the twenty-first century.

Structure of AYSO

The organization is governed by a board of directors and the national president, all of them volunteers. Working closely with the board of directors is the staff at the National Support Center in Hawthorne, California. Here, a multitude of services are provided for the membership: training support for coaches and referees; local volunteer administrators; data processing and accounting services; accident reimbursement; risk management; tournaments; cultural exchange information; recognition programs; marketing and sponsorship acquisition; and educational seminars.

The grassroots level of AYSO starts with a community-based league, known as a region. Each region is headed by a regional commissioner. Regional commissioners have the responsibility and authority to conduct the business of the region within the framework of AYSO's philosophy and the national rules and regulations and bylaws. Depending on its stage of development, a region might have as few as 12 or as many as 400 teams, grouped for competition into boys and girls divisions by age. VIP divisions for children with special needs exist in many regions as well.

Area directors supervise several regions yet recognize local autonomy. Area directors are responsible for the performance and growth in their areas. Section directors are responsible for the general welfare and administration of a section that consists of a number of areas.

Members of the board of directors, section directors, area directors, and regional commissioners are executive members and thereby are the voting members of AYSO.

This is the team. From the local region to the national board, all of AYSO recognizes the value of a healthy competitive environment where children can grow and develop through soccer. It's all fun and it's all AYSO!

Glossary of Youth Soccer Terms

Advantage   A clause in the rules that permits the referee to refrain from stopping play for a foul if the team that was fouled already has possession of the ball and is in a good attacking position. However, if the advantage does not ensue then the referee may stop play and penalize the fouling team.

Assist   A play in which one player passes to another, who scores.

Attacker   A forward or striker.

Attacking team   The team that has possession of the ball.

AYSO   American Youth Soccer Organization.

Back   A defender.

Beat   To get the ball past an opponent by dribbling, passing, or shooting.

Behind the defender   In the area between a defender and the defender's goal.

Break   A play in which a team quickly advances the ball down the field before the opposition has a chance to retreat.

Caution   See "Yellow card."

Center   A cross, or pass, from a player located near the sideline toward the middle of the field; used to get the ball closer to the front of the goal.

Central defender   A player who plays in the middle of defense, directly in front of his or her goalkeeper.

Clear   To kick the ball away from the area near one's goal.

Cleats   The metal, plastic, or rubber studs in the bottom of a soccer boot used to provide traction; also used to refer to the boots themselves.

Club   A team that plays in a league.

Control   A play in which 2 player uses his or her body—chest, thighs, hands, or feet—to stop a moving ball.

Counterattack   An attack launched by a defending team soon after it regains possession of the ball.

Creating space   Moving away from a teammate with the ball in order to draw defenders from the ball carrier and so give him or her space.

Cross   See "Center."

Dangerous play   Any action which the referee considers to be dangerous. For example: A player attempting to kick a head-height ball when an opposing player is challenging for the ball by attempting to head it.

Defenders   Backs—fullbacks, center backs, stopper, and sweeper.

Defending team   The team that does not have possession of the ball.

Deflection   The ricochet of a ball after it hits a player, post, or referee.

Diving header   A ball struck by the head of a diving player.

Draw   A game that ends with a tied score.

Dropped ball   A way of restarting the game. The referee drops the ball between two players facing each other.

Drop kick   A kick in which a goalie kicks the ball from his or her penalty area by dropping it from the hands and kicking it just as it hits the ground.

Endline   See "Goal line."

Extra time   See "Overtime."

Fake   A "dummy" move meant to deceive an opposing player; used by a ball carrier to make a defender think the ball carrier is going to dribble, pass, or shoot in a certain direction when he or she is not.

Far post   The goalpost furthest from the ball.

Feint   See "Fake."

Football   Name for soccer in most countries outside the United States.

Formation   The arrangement of players on the field; for example, in 11-a-side soccer, a 4-4-2 formation is one in which a team is playing with 1 goalkeeper, 4 defenders, 4 midfielders, and 2 forwards. (The goalkeeper is not listed in the formation since every formation plays with just one goalkeeper.)

Forwards   The attackers, strikers, and wingers on the team, who are responsible for most of the scoring.

Foul   A violation of the rules for which an official assesses a free kick or a penalty kick.

Fullbacks   Defenders who play near the touch lines. There are two—a left back and a right back.

Goal kick   A way of restarting the game when the ball that crossed the goal line was last touched by an attacking player. The ball is kicked from anywhere inside the goal area.

Goal line   The line on which the goal stands.

Goal mouth   The front opening to each goal.

Halfback   An outdated term. See "Midfielders."

Halftime   The intermission between the two periods, or halves, of a game.

Hand ball   A foul in which a player other than the goalie touches the ball with his or her hand or arm.

Hat trick   Three goals scored in a game by a single player.

Injury time   Time added on to the end of any half because of time lost due to player injuries, substitutions, or intentional delays by a team.

In play   Referring to a ball that is within the boundaries of the field, if play has not been stopped by the referee.

Linesmen   The assistant referees who patrol the touch lines.

Lob   See "Loft."

Loft   A high-arcing kick.

Marking   Guarding a player to prevent him from passing or receiving the ball.

Match   A soccer game.

Midfield   The region of the field near the center line; the area controlled by the midfielders.

Midfielders   The players who link together the attacking and defensive functions of a team. They play between the forwards and the defenders.

Near post   The goalpost closest to the ball.

Net   The mesh draped over the frame of the goal to catch the ball when a goal is scored.

Obstruction   A play in which a defensive player uses his or her body to prevent an offensive player from playing the ball.

Offensive player   See "Attacker."

Offensive team   See "Attacking team."

Officials The referee and two or three assistant referees who officiate a game of soccer.

Offside   A violation called when a player in an *offside position* (see term) receives a pass or interferes with play from a teammate.

Offside position   A play in which an attacking player is positioned in his opponent's half with fewer than two opposing defensive players (usually the goalie and one other defender) between him and the goal he is attacking when he receives the ball.

On-side   The opposite of offside.

Open   Referring to a player who does not have anyone *marking* (see term) him or her.

Out of bounds   Referring to a situation in which a ball is outside the boundaries of the field.

Out of play   See "Out of bounds."

Overtime   The periods played after regulation in a game that ended tied.

Penalty   Short for "penalty kick" (see term); also, a punishment given by the referee when a defending player commits a direct free kick foul within the penalty area.

Penalty kick   A kick taken from the penalty mark by a player against the opposing goalie.

Pitch   A British term for "soccer field."

Play on   An instruction used by referees to indicate that advantage has been applied.

Possession   Control of the ball.

Post   Goalpost.

Red card   A card that a referee holds up to signal that a player has been sent off. He could be removed for other reasons—injury for instance.

Referee   The chief official at a game.

Regular season   The schedule of games played before a playoff is held.

Save   The act of a goalkeeper in blocking or stopping a shot on goal.

Score   To put the ball into the net for a goal; the tally of goals during a game.

Scorers   Players who score goals.

Screening   See "Shielding."

Set play   A planned play from a "dead-ball situation" such as a corner kick or free kick.

Shielding   Protect the ball from a defender by keeping one's body between the ball and the defender.

Shin guards   Shin pads that protect the front of a player's legs.

Shooting   Kicking the ball at the opponent's net in an attempt to score a goal.

Short-sided game   A game played with fewer than 11 players per side.

Shot   A ball kicked or headed at the opponent's net in an attempt to score a goal.

Shutout   A team prevents the opposition from scoring any goals in a game.

Sideline   The line that runs along the length of the field on each side.

Sliding tackle   A play in which the player slides on the ground feet-first to tackle an opposing player who has possession of the ball.

Small-sided game   See "Short-sided game."

Square pass   A pass made by one player to a teammate alongside him or her.

Stopper   The defender that marks an opposing striker with the aim of stopping him or her from scoring.

Striker   A team's primary scorer.

Substitution   Replacement of one player on the field with another player not on the field.

Sweeper   The defender that plays closest to his or her own goal behind the rest of the defenders; a team's last line of defense in front of the goalkeeper.

Touch line   See "Sideline."

Trap   See "Control."

USYSA   United States Youth Soccer Association.

Volley   A ball kicked by a player before it hits the ground.

Wall   A line of defending players standing together to protect their goal against a close free kick.

Wingers   The attacking players who play along the *wings* (see term) with the aim of crossing the ball in to the forwards.

Wings   The areas of the field closest to the touch lines.

World Cup   The international soccer competition for the men's and women's teams held by FIFA every four years between the top national teams in the world.

Yellow card   A card that a referee holds up to indicate that a player has been cautioned. Two yellow cards in one game earns a player an automatic red card, signaling the player's removal from the game.

Index

boys' teams, separate, 122
bruising, 160
buildup play, 88–92

calves, stretches for, 157
camaraderie, development of,
    32–33, 140
caring, 176
casts, disallowed on field, 71
catching, goalkeeper's skill of,
    61, 100–101
caution, signal for, 199
    See also yellow cards
center backs, in 4-4-2
    formation, 43
center mark, 65
changing pace, 52, 106
character, 173–78
    caring and, 176
    citizenship and, 176–77
    conflict and, 177
    defined, 174–75
    fairness and, 176
    hints for teaching, 177–78
    respect and, 175
    responsibility and, 175–76
    six pillars of, 175
    trustworthiness and, 175
charitable work, 32
Chastain, Brandi, 203, 224, 225
cheating, 176
chest, ball control with, 53, 90
child protection, Safe Haven
    program for, 181, 226
chip pass, 107–8
citizenship, 176–77
clearance, 62, 101
clothing, 69–71, 169
Coach Certification program,
    226
coaches:
    aptitude testing for, 145–46
    assistant, 148
    conscience of, 142
    cooperation with, 210
    expectations of, 141
    good example set by, 23,
        143–44
    honesty of, 147

how to be, 146–47
as instructing without
    condemning, 23
key points for, 138–45
meetings of parents and, 66,
    148–54
mistakes of, 145
problems with, 153–54
sideline, parents as, 165–66
special situations for, 154
teamwork developed by, 30–32
time volunteered by, 170
coaching, 138–62
    injuries and, 160–62
    positive, 18, 22–23, 143
    of practice sessions, 155–59
    praising the individual but
        correcting the group in, 23,
        29
coaching areas, seating in, 183
coed teams, 122
coin toss, 74, 191
cold packs, 159
commitment, 26–27, 33–34
common sense, law of, 188
compassion, 176
competition:
    clean and fair, 71, 170
    rising above, 177
compression, for injuries, 161
CONCACAF (Confederation of
    North, Central American,
    and Caribbean Association
    Football), 223–24
concentration, 38, 88
concussion, 162
conflict of interest, 187–88
consistency, 176
control, *see* ball control
cool-down, 159
cooperation, 25, 210
corner, 96–97
    far-post, 99
    near-post, 97
corner arc, 67
corner kicks, 67, 76, 81, 86
    positioning at, 193
    for U-6 age group, 125
    for U-8 age group, 130

ABOUT THE AUTHORS

VINCENT FORTANASCE, M.D., is a neurologist, psychiatrist, and youth sports expert. He is also a devoted soccer dad and coach. He lives in Pasadena, California.

LAWRENCE ROBINSON writes about soccer for *Gear* and other magazines and has played soccer for fifteen years. He lives in Los Angeles, California.

JOHN OUELLETTE has been the AYSO National Coach for the past thirteen years. A former head soccer coach for Weber State University in Utah, he has canvassed the country, offering personal training to AYSO coaches. He lives in Fruit Heights, Utah.

PARENT-TESTED AND AYSO APPROVED

Good-natured guidance for teaching children the long-term benefits of playing youth soccer

LIFE LESSONS FROM SOCCER

WHAT YOUR CHILD CAN LEARN ON AND OFF THE FIELD

A Guide for Parents & Coaches

VINCENT FORTANASCE, M.D.

0-7432-0575-8 • October 2001 • $13.00

FIRESIDE

www.simonsays.com